Library of
Davidson College

A Woman's Money
*How to Protect and Increase It
in the Stock Market*

A Woman's Money
How to Protect and Increase It in the Stock Market

Catharine Brandt

Parker Publishing Company, Inc.
West Nyack, N.Y.

© 1970 by

PARKER PUBLISHING COMPANY, INC.
West Nyack, New York

ALL RIGHTS RESERVED. NO PART
OF THIS BOOK MAY BE REPRODUCED
IN ANY FORM, OR BY ANY MEANS,
WITHOUT PERMISSION IN WRITING
FROM THE PUBLISHER.

Library of Congress
Catalog Card Number: 72-91992

This publication is designed to provide accurate and authoritative information with regard to the subject matter covered. It is sold with the understanding that the publisher is not engaged in rendering legal, accounting, or other professional advice. If legal advice or other expert assistance is required, the services of a competent professional person should be sought.

—From a Declaration of Principles jointly adopted by a Committee of the American Bar Association and a Committee of Publishers and Associations

PRINTED IN THE UNITED STATES OF AMERICA

B & P–13-962258-6

To
RUSS
who started it all

What You Can Expect from This Book

The signs of the times point to stormy financial weather ahead. What we women need today is an umbrella—something to protect us from the soaring cost of living and taxes.

Careful, informed investment in common stocks holds such protection.

To understand sensible investing takes work, of course. I didn't understand everything all at once. But a woman *can* have an exciting time learning. In the process she can become aware of how increased capital will protect her both in the present and in the future, how it will help finance her obligations to herself, her family, the church, and others in need.

The advice and methods offered here have been tried and tested not only by various women, including the author, but also by highly successful male investors. This book focuses on how you can protect and increase your money. I believe you can do this by becoming an informed common stock *investor,* not a *speculator.*

You don't need a degree in accounting or business administration to put the methods in this book to work.

You can begin the same way I did:
- Not very good at math
- Not much interested in the stock market
- Dependent on someone else to protect my money

You can wind up like thousands of women have:
- Understanding the stock market
- Making money in the stock market
- Protecting and increasing your money

Before you say you haven't the money to spare for common stock investing, study some of the real-life examples in this book. You'll find you don't need a lot of money to start. The important thing is to *begin* to invest. The money you invest now can work for you, increasing 7 percent, or 10 or 15 percent, a year. The dividends your stock pays can add to your present income, or you can use them to buy more stock.

The key to increasing your capital is to read each chapter carefully and then act upon the suggestions at the end of the chapter. Just by figuring out the answers to the questions at end of Chapter 1 you will be better able to manage your money. Setting up a trial portfolio as explained in Chapter 2 will prevent blunders and give you confidence when you actually begin to invest.

What you will read in these pages is based on two premises:

First, the idea, not original with me, that America's increasing population, higher standards of living, and the affluence of great numbers of people, create a continuing high demand for goods and services. All this turns the wheels of American business and hoists the price of common stocks.

Second, the idea that women can learn how to protect and increase their money in the stock market if they set their mind to it.

Don't consider any of the stocks named as a recommendation to buy. They are used merely as examples because they are stocks familiar to me. Also, don't think that this book contains everything that can be said about investing. But you will, I'm sure, refer to it again and again. After reading it you will be far more knowledgeable about the stock market and investing than before. What's more, you will have confidence to make your own selections of common stock.

Reading this book and acting on the suggestions can be the start of something big for you.

Catharine Brandt

Contents

1. **Your Money Can Earn Profits for You** 15

    Know What Inflation Means (16) Investing in Common Stocks Can Be the Answer (17) Managing Your Income Is a Lifetime Job (18) First Things First (20) Pay Yourself First (22) Women as Shareholders (23) Preparation for Investing (24) The Way to Take Off (25) You Don't Need to Be Rich (26)

2. **Use a Trial Portfolio** 29

    Getting Ready to Play the Game (30) Rules of the Game (32) Risk (35) Some Pitfalls That Can Cause Trouble (36) What a Beginner Can Expect (38) Profit Margin (39) Sample Trial Portfolio (39)

3. **Where to Get Help** 42

    Learn to Study (43) Special Helps (43) Visit a Brokerage Office (49) Amount Invested (50) Intuition, Sentiment and "Hot" Tips (51)

4. **Picking Up the Jargon** 54

5. **How the Stock Market Functions** 76

    What the Stock Market Is (78) Gross National Product (79) Shareholders' Part (80) How It All Began (81) How the Stock Market Functions (81) New York Stock Exchange (83) American Stock Exchange (83) Over-the-Counter Market (83) Mechanics of Buying and Selling (84) What About Safety? (86) Protection of Securities and Exchange Commission (87) Why the Market Fluctuates (88)

6. **How to Read a Financial Report** 90

    Improved Format Helpful (91) What to Look For (92) President Chats with Shareholders (98) Back to the Balance Sheet (99) A

Look at the Income Statement (100) You've Invited to the Annual Meeting (104)

7. What You Can Learn from Investment Clubs 107

What the NAIC Offers You (107) NAIC Guidelines (109) How to Start a Club (109) Call the First Meeting (110) Second Meeting (111) Help from NAIC (113) Club Officers (113) Committees (114) NAIC Formula (115) Minimum Standards of NAIC (117) Investigate Thoroughly (117)

8. How to Evaluate a Company 119

How to Choose a Winner (120) Look at Your Neighbors (120) Invest for the Long Haul (121) Invest in Growth Stocks (122) What Do the Experts Mean When They Talk About Growth Stocks? (123) Don't Be Enticed by Low Price (124) Fashions in Stocks (125) Invest in Quality (128) Protect Your Money by Diversification (130) Invest Regularly (131) Timing (132) Review Your Holdings (132) Professional Yardstick (133) When to Sell (134) How Do You Find a Winner? (135)

9. Final Check-Up Before You Buy 137

Money to Invest (137) Long-Range Plan (137) Questions to Ask Yourself (138) Choose a Listed Stock (139) Is the Price Right? (139) Timing (140) Avoid Procrastination (141) Choose a Broker and Open an Account (142) Unscrupulous Brokers (143) Spread Your Investment (143) Register Your Stock (143) You Might Try a Formula (144) Final Check (146)

10. What You Should Know About Trusts and Mutual Funds 149

Something Less Than Success (151) Here Is How It Worked (152) Look Before You Buy (154) Types and Terms to Understand (154) Funds Would Like to Manage Your Money (156) What Makes Mutual Funds Popular? (157) What Price Performance? (162)

11. Getting Your Money's Worth When You Buy Mutual Funds ... 164

Where to Find Out About Funds (165) Facts to Help You Choose the Right Fund (166) Net Asset Value (168) The Importance of Finding the Right Fund (168) Seven Ways to Test the Fund You Are Interested In (169) Funds Under Federal In-

vestigation (171) Points to Check Before You Buy (172) Questions to Ponder if You Want to Get Your Money's Worth (174)

12. Keeping Essential Records 176

Certificates in Street Name (176) Advantages of Placing Certificates in Street Name (177) Disadvantages of Leaving Certificates in Street Name (178) Be Professional by Keeping These Minimum Records (180) Certificates in Your Own Name (182) What You Need to Keep Your Own Records (182)

13. The Art of Giving 186

The Importance of Understanding Facts About Gifts (188) Ways to Make Contributions That Will Benefit You (190)

14. What to Do About Your Income Tax 197

Report Your Income Accurately (197) Proper Ways to Reduce Your Income Tax (198) How to Figure Cost Base on Your Stocks (199) How You Can Gain by End-of-Year Sales (200) Be Sure to Take Advantage of These Deductions (201) Non-Business Deductions (203) Importance of a Will (204) Joint Ownership (204) Estate Taxes Can Be Reduced (205) Further Tips (206) Single Women at a Tax Disadvantage (207)

15. Beyond Profits 209

Shares Sold to Pay for Revolutionary War (210) America's First Stock Exchange (210) The Great Crash (211) Securities and Exchange Acts (212) Trading Shares in Early Days (212) The Curb or AMEX (213) Wall Street (213) Legendary Terms (214) Modern Touch (214)

Bibliography 219

A Woman's Money
How to Protect and Increase It

in the Stock Market

Your Money Can Earn Profits for You   1

When you talk to some women about saving money for the future, chances are you'll hit that pocketbook nerve. Just mention investing in stocks and you'll meet with resistance or a blank stare. I know. I was one who resisted and stared.

Marion Lewis is another. "Tom's take-home pay is only $100 a week," she says. "We're broke three days before pay day. How can anyone save for the future when things cost so much?"

Sandra McKelvey's husband died a few years ago, leaving her with $30,000 in life insurance. Sandra, because of her husband-sheltered years, thought she had a fortune. The next year she toured Europe, then put the rest of the money in a savings account.

"I'll have the insurance money to live on when I retire," she said. When spring came, even though she had a clerking job, Sandra drew on the insurance to pay for a new car. Staring her in the face now is the knowledge that her money may not last as long as she does.

"Dabbling in the stock market is gambling," Tess Whitcomb declares. "Margin and all that. My uncle filed for bankruptcy because he played the stock market. I'm putting my money in the bank where it will be safe." Like many other women, Tess fails to understand that intelligent investing in stocks can in the long flight protect her money in a way the bank does not—higher growth of capital.

The names are fictitious, but daily countless women enact the same real-life drama.

KNOW WHAT INFLATION MEANS

Because of inflation, settled around our shoulders like a mink stole, some lessons about money we women learned when growing up must be unlearned. Money in the sock can be stolen. Money in the bank does not grow as fast as the economy. When you come to spend it the money may not be worth as much as when you put it in the bank.

Here's why. A thousand dollars deposited in the savings bank or in government savings bonds ten years ago would now be increased by interest. But because of the rising cost of living you would have to open your purse and add several hundred dollars in order to buy what you might have bought ten years ago.

From 1960 through 1965 prices consumers paid for goods and services rose around 2 percent a year. In 1968 prices for the same goods and services jumped more than 4 percent, biggest annual gain since 1951. Your money, then, must be invested to compound at a rate at least equal to the increase of more than 4 percent a year, in order just to hold your own. Besides, the increase must be great enough to cover income taxes.

One way to understand this troublesome statistic is to look at the Consumer Price Index (CPI). The index covers all goods and services that people buy. With the average figured at 100 for the years 1957 to 1959, the CPI rose to 113.1 in 1966, and to a startling 121 in 1968. If you paid $100 for a watch in 1957, you would pay $121 or more for the same watch today, exclusive of any sales tax. This applies to almost anything you may buy.

Thus any fixed payments you count on for the future, such as annuities, insurance, pensions, and government savings bonds (all good and basic ways to save money) do not provide enough interest to offset the rising cost of living.

How can we women combat the dollar loss in fixed savings and income? How can we conserve and protect our capital, and even increase it for retirement years?

INVESTING IN COMMON STOCKS CAN BE THE ANSWER

Today over 26,000,000 Americans own shares of stock, 52 percent of them women. Before you conclude that these women must all be wealthy, listen to this result of a recent New York Stock Exchange survey: 55 percent of all shareowners reported annual household incomes of less than $10,000, and 20 percent have incomes below $5,000.

Women who, like Tess Whitcomb, believe that buying stocks involves gambling should understand that the stock market is a part of the American economy and that *investing* is very different from gambling. Many new business ventures would never take off but for the savings of hundreds of persons who own shares in such corporations. Great research projects would probably never get off the launching pad without such financial assistance.

This should not surprise us too much, for which one of us has not on occasion borrowed money for installment buying? Or to charge goods for a month or three? Putting money in the bank is lending it.

Besides women who openly resist the idea of buying stocks, many others with enough firsthand experience with the rising cost of living to make them uneasy about the future are asking questions. Perhaps you have a sum of money to invest and have wondered about the stock market. All you need is a push in the right direction.

I'm glad I was pushed. Some years ago my husband, knowledgeable about investing in stocks, said to me, "You ought to learn about the stock market. It would be a good hobby for you."

My answer was a groan and a grimace. Being good at figures was not my chief talent. What did I know about those columns of tiny figures on the business page of the newspaper? Nothing, except that my husband had bought some of our stocks in my name, and I had the fun of cashing the dividend checks. Couldn't I just invest without a lot of work? Why should I read up on the stock market? To do so would mean studying the unknown, and I was busy with other projects. But his suggestions needled me. Was I turning my back on opportunity by refusing to learn from the expert I knew my husband to be? Would the time come when I would wish I understood the rudiments of stock investing?

Soon I changed my mind and began to study. Library books, financial columns and stock quotations, financial magazines, Dow Jones Industrials, New York and American Stock Exchanges all came up for probing. Before long I found myself smack in the middle of an exciting learning adventure. Now I'm hooked. What started out to be a hobby has turned into a profitable adventure.

MANAGING YOUR INCOME IS A LIFETIME JOB

Since women, I soon learned, control more than half of America's wealth, they need to understand how to conserve income and capital. Because wives more often than not hold the checkbook, they are responsible for saving as well as spending. Again, women as a rule live five to ten years longer than their husbands, so that widows frequently find themselves in charge of substantial sums of money. A small estate takes hanging onto with both hands to protect it.

Single women especially must plan for the years ahead. A survey shows that women's salaries are 5 percent to 44 percent less than those of men for comparable jobs. In addition, women need extra income to offset somewhat discriminatory income taxes which at present are levied against the single person. A husband and wife, for instance, can file separate returns and split the income tax rate, thereby receiving more favorable tax treatment than the widow or single woman.

Something that most of us ignore or forget is adequate planning for the future. We spend money now that we will need 30 or 40 years from now in retirement. Many women shop carefully for household expenses. They look for food and drug buys and compare prices on slacks and shoes. They strive to make their husband's or their own pay check go as far as possible. But when it comes to thinking about the future or saving for retirement, they shrug.

"I leave all that to Jim," one wife says. "He doesn't know the first thing about decorating or shopping for groceries so he leaves that to me. But he does know about investing so I leave all that to him."

Of course this is a practical arrangement if you can be sure Jim will live as long as you do. We women, though, can't depend on having a man to take charge of our affairs as long as we live.

If you have never thought much about what your future income will be or how you will protect and conserve your capital, why not get the picture of your whole life? You may think retirement is as remote as scheduled interplanetary travel. Would you believe that right now in the United States nearly nine million persons are over 75, and more than a million are over 85? More and more women retire at 62 instead of 65. If the trend continues even earlier retirement will result, and this in turn will require more capital.

Life, you might say, divides into three parts:

- From birth to the end of school years, or about age 22
- The years you earn a living, about age 22 to 62
- Retirement to death, about age 62 to ?

It's amazing how naively some women look at the future, women who otherwise are knowledgeable about current expenses. Last summer over coffee several women talked about retirement plans. Georgia Swanson (not her real name) said, "Who's worrying? Our house is paid for. We'll have social security and medicare." The rest of us sat stunned, knowing that social security payments would not be enough.

Or take the elderly couple who long ago bought a $500 insurance policy to "bury us with," they said. It doesn't take a slide rule to figure out that someone will have to add to that amount when the time comes.

May Kinney, a single woman recently retired, states, "For a long time I based my future plans on the $100 a month pension check I would receive after I retired. Years ago $100 plus social security meant a fair monthly income for a woman alone. But not now. I firmly believe that for women with fixed income like me, the only chance to make money is in the stock market. My investments have already proved profitable."

The woman who invests her money in well-managed, growing American industries makes an investment in America's future as well as her own. She can expect her capital to grow far above the rising economy or cost of living.

Should every woman invest? A small percentage of women have no business in the stock market. Their nature, attitudes, capabilities, and lack of capital make it doubtful they should invest in common stock, at least until changes occur. But most women can manage and increase their money just as well as a man can. It takes work, of course, to understand and pursue a sensible investment plan, but you can have a good time learning and working, and can expect profits in the end.

FIRST THINGS FIRST

No matter how ready you consider yourself for investing in the stock market, you should take into account the various types of investments and understand the ones you need before jumping into the market.

1. Savings accounts

Money placed in a bank savings account and allowed to remain there at 4 percent interest compounded quarterly will double your capital in about 18 years. (Divide the rate of interest into the number 72 to arrive at the approximate time it will take your money compounded to double.) Long-term savings certificates, usually for $1,000 or multiples of that amount, pay a little over 5 percent interest, either directly to you semi-annually, or compounded.

2. Bonds

The government—local, state, federal—and corporations issue bonds for the purpose of borrowing money. Bonds bear interest paid at stated intervals, or in the case of some United States savings bonds, at maturity.

3. Insurance

Money invested in life insurance is protection for the future. In addition the cash value of the policy can be borrowed at less interest usually than borrowing from a bank. Adequate health, injury, and property insurance allow people to invest more money because they need less cash reserve for emergencies.

4. Real estate

Money invested in real estate does increase in value in times of inflation, but often decreases in depressions. It may also decrease in value because of shifting neighborhood conditions. Real estate takes additional capital for taxes and upkeep, both of which increase with the age of the property. Real estate also entails a certain amount of supervision. If you are one of those on the move from city to city, or state to state, you may find when you get ready to sell that a limited or unfavorable market exists. In the case of the house you live in, if you sell at an inflated price and buy another house, you will doubtless buy at an inflated price. For a family, though, owning a home is one of the best protections against an uncertain future.

5. Common stocks

The woman who invests in common stocks becomes a part owner of the company whose shares she buys (albeit a very small part owner). If the company has reverses, she stands to lose money. If the company experiences growth and expansion, increased sales and profits, she can expect to share in this. Usually she will receive regular dividends and the value of her stock will go up, not remain static or fixed. Though the stock market does fluctuate, the trend has, over the years, been steadily upward, and spectacularly upward in many good growth stocks; more about these later.

Young women usually think they need all their income for the day-to-day tussle, and even older women feel the same. Mrs. Carter, whose husband retires in five years, is doing nothing about setting aside funds for their so-near future. Saving must compete with the pull of advertising, the stores filled with beautiful merchandise—and money is to spend, isn't it?

As a young woman you are perhaps thinking, "I would never wait that long. Five years before retirement!" But the older woman, whose husband earns a high salary, may still make better provision than the young woman who never sets a pattern for regular saving for the future.

PAY YOURSELF FIRST

Budget experts counsel us to "pay yourself first." That is, set aside a definite percentage of your pay check each pay day and bank it as regularly as you pay other bills. The next time you get a raise, or your income tax refund check, or any windfall, how about buying shares of stock? Can you cut a corner and come up with something left over each month or even each quarter? When you understand the amount of true interest you pay on major appliances, TV, or even your car, sometimes 15 percent or more, you will struggle out of such non-profit quagmires. But even if getting your hands on extra money now looks impossible because providing for current expenses, insurance, and emergency funds takes all your pay, you can learn right now the big place investing in common stocks can have in your future. Such knowledge is more than likely to prove helpful later.

Before reading on, why not do a little homework? Spread open the financial page of your newspaper.

1. Read the short news article on the stock market's performance for the day. Read any stock column article.
2. Check the Dow Jones industrial average. Check Standard and Poor's averages and the New York Stock Exchange average.
3. Look at the list of the ten or fifteen most active stocks for the day. Do you recognize the abbreviations as names of companies you know?
4. Look at the headings for the reports of the New York and the American Stock Exchanges—high, low, last, change.
5. Read what the code letters at the end of the stock quotations stand for, such as a, xr, and z.
6. Scan the quotations of over-the-counter stocks and investment funds.

Write down any questions you have. For instance, you may wonder what the Dow Jones average is and what over-the-counter stocks are. You will find such questions answered later or refer to Chapter 4, Picking Up the Jargon.

WOMEN AS SHAREHOLDERS

One investment counselor advises each of his clients to buy some shares of stock in his wife's name. Even two or three shares, he says, get a woman interested in the stock market.

Suppose a woman's husband dies and leaves her an estate of $100,000, not uncommon today when you add up house, personal property, car, savings, and insurance. A woman who found herself in this situation says, "Both of us worked hard all our lives, and I would feel dishonest if I spent all that money for *fun*! I want to conserve it for our children and grandchildren."

Or imagine a retired school teacher whose father dies, leaving her a multiple unit apartment building, old and in need of repair. She has neither the physical strength nor the inclination to oversee this property. How much better for her to sell the apartment building and buy high-grade, income-producing stocks, which she can oversee and manage from her own desk right in her home.

PREPARATION FOR INVESTING

How can you best prepare yourself for investing in the stock market? Many a college graduate winds up knowing little about managing her own finances or investing. But if you have kept careful household records and operated your finances in the black, you may have a sound basis for becoming a successful investor. To run a house or manage your pay check takes business skill. It takes accurate bookkeeping and records for income tax returns. It entails writing checks, paying bills, searching for value in purchases, deciding what necessities and what luxuries to buy, and saving for the future. These skills prepare you for careful investing.

Some women, though, realizing they are rusty in basic math and simple bookkeeping, take an adult refresher course before wading into the stock market. This helps to understand percentages, fractions, interest, and bookkeeping. Such a course can be studied at any business school or adult education class offered at night in many city high schools. Or you may review on your own as I did.

A good book for home study is *Decimals and Percentages,* by Betty Friel. A self-help book, it allows the student to progress at her own speed. Because the questions interlock, you must come up with the right answer to the question studied before proceeding to the next one.

THE WAY TO TAKE OFF

It's best to understand at the outset that this book will not tell you how to make a million dollars overnight or even over a lifetime. If you're looking for "hot" tips you won't find them here. The only way to learn about stocks is to read up on established progressive companies in news articles, financial reports, and company prospectuses (in which a company spreads out its finances for all to see). You can also visit a brokerage house for advice, asking to read papers on any company you are considering for investment.

Success stories of persons making $10,000 in the stock market in a few days or weeks by buying some highly speculative stock are told because they are uncommon and they make fascinating reading. Most of us would like to see more checks coming our way and our shares increasing in value. Common stock, however, should be bought only after careful research and study of:

- A woman's income, financial habits, objectives
- The merits of the company under consideration
- The condition of the market at the time

The New York Stock Exchange alone lists nearly 1,300 companies. Hundreds of them are well-known firms. Others are comparatively new, with progressive ideas. They have yet to prove that they can make money for their stockholders. These corporations all need capital with which to promote research programs, buy additions to their businesses, or expand in other ways. Still other firms are classed as speculative. Whether they will become sound corporations is anybody's guess. Speculation can occasionally bring great rewards. It can also cause you to lose money. For this reason, speculative stock holds too much risk for the woman just beginning to invest.

Security advisors point out that a woman should invest in stocks only after she has made provision for current needs, emergencies, and insurance. Something else to understand is that a woman should not buy common stock unless she can spare the money for several years. It takes a period of time for any stockholder to gain the best profits from his shares.

If you are one of those who might regret stock purchases at every market drop by crying, "Why didn't I put my money in the bank where it would be safe?" you should understand that money in the bank is indeed safer than money in stocks with one small difference. It may not buy as much when you are ready to spend it as it would have bought when you deposited it in the bank.

The only success story for the woman with a small amount to invest is common sense in choosing stock and the patience to sit back and wait for the stock to produce.

YOU DON'T NEED TO BE RICH

Perhaps by now you're ready to close this book and exclaim, "All that talk about stocks is for rich women. I don't have any money to invest." Think again about the statistics that more than 50 percent of all stockholders have incomes of $5,000 to $10,000. You don't need a four-figure sum to invest in common stocks. Don't let the fact that you have only a small amount to invest deter you. The Monthly Investment Plan of the New York Stock Exchange allows you to invest as little as $40 a quarter. (More of this later.)

Perhaps you work for a firm that has a stock-sharing plan whereby the company matches or provides at a special rate shares of stock for the employee to buy. One young woman says about the plan her husband's employer provides, "We wouldn't own one share of stock if it weren't for the company. They give us one free share for every share we buy.

It's too good an offer to pass up even if it means doing without something we want now."

For the woman whose husband carries adequate insurance to protect her and the children in case of his sudden death, whose savings account holds cash for an emergency equal to two months' pay, who has some reserve in government savings bonds, is making payments on a home, and paying bills promptly, investing regularly in stocks can be a fine protection for the future.

For single women or widows, protection for others may not be so important, but the burden for the future falls squarely on your shoulders.

At first all this may make you uneasy. Suppose you are one of those with wall-to-wall bills, and also in the $5,000 to $10,000 income bracket. Why not scrutinize your cost to live? If others can invest, why can't you? The answer may lie in retreating instead of charging so much. Can you subtract something from your regular expenses and save a little each month? Savings rate a high priority in any woman's management of her finances. Perhaps you must start with only a few dollars a week or a month, but the amount should be paid as surely as you pay the rent.

Those who think about the future make a place in the family budget for savings. In all this planning moral and spiritual values pop up. Making a goal of security will find us the losers. Obligations to those in need in the world also face us. My husband believed that money was a trust from God. So he taught me to protect it and to try to increase it, not only for our own benefit, but for our children, our church, and those in need in the world.

Here is where intelligent buying of common stocks enters. As America's economy increases, so will our capital.

To Benefit Most from This Chapter: Answer the Following Questions:

1. How many years before your retirement?

2. What income will you have at retirement age, whether your husband is living or you are a widow or single?
3. Will your expected income cover retirement expenses?
4. What are your monthly expenses today?
5. What income will you have should your husband die prematurely? This year? Five years from now? Ten?
6. Will this income be adequate?
7. What is your present income?
8. Will this income be adequate if the cost of living continues to rise?

Use a Trial Portfolio   2

For the woman who knows little about investing in stocks but would like to know more, making a hypothetical portfolio may help, as it helped me. In investment circles, *portfolio* means the securities held by an investor. Don't let the term *hypothetical* bother you. It's just a make-believe game you played as a child.

Even college business administration classes today play the game. In one Minnesota University investment class, students each received $1,000 (make-believe, of course) to invest. The class divided into several groups, pooled resources and knowledge, and hopped into the market. At the close of the quarter each group reported on its successes and losses. The trial run revealed that some groups made money while others lost. All had received the same classroom instruction, but some investigated and deliberated more carefully than others.

At another college a student reports that one of her professors required the class to study different corporations. Each student looked up the earnings record of the company assigned to her. After discussion the class voted on the stock most likely to succeed, pooled their money (actual cash), and bought four shares. At the end of the year they sold the stock and pocketed the profits.

"I had my eyes opened," the girl says, "to the importance of investigating before investing. That class got me started buying shares on my own."

A women's investment club in Duluth played the same game with $10,000 (imaginary). Each woman chose her own stocks, and bought and sold as she wished. The group kept a record of companies, prices and sales. Six months later the women computed the results of their hypothetical portfolios and awarded a prize to the one who "made" the most money. A learning experience they all agreed.

GETTING READY TO PLAY THE GAME

Let's pretend you have $5,000 to invest in the stock market. You don't need that much to begin investing, but $5,000 is a nice round figure to illustrate some of the fundamentals of safe investing. Suppose you have $5,000 you want to put aside for future use—education of the children, that once-in-a-lifetime trip, down payment on a house, retirement income. Some goals might not use all the $5,000, but others would probably cost a great deal more. You want the money to work for you and when you begin to use it, you want a good return, or interest through the years.

Will you buy blue chip stocks, so named because of their long record of paying dividends and their steady growth in value through the years? American Telephone and Telegraph Company, General Motors, General Electric are examples.

Or will you buy stock in growth companies that have enjoyed spectacular increases the last few years? Such companies pay little or no dividends, turning the profits back into the company. Examples might be Control Data, Texas Instruments. The woman who owned shares in one of these companies from the time it began to grow will get a fine prize when she sells and takes her profits.

In setting up your trial portfolio, decide on four or five different industries you believe might play an important part in our country's future progress. You might think of airlines, chemicals, clothing, food, natural gas, oil. Your reasoning might be that because of increased population at home and

Use a Trial Portfolio

abroad, all these industries will have to increase production. True enough. But in order for you to make money in the stock market, your *shares* must increase in value. Some of the above industries grow faster than others. Watching them for a time on a trial portfolio basis will help you see this.

Next make a list of two or three corporations in each industry. Think of well-known companies advertised in magazines, or located in your city, or whose products you use and like.

Familiarity is not the only measurement. I remember when my trial portfolio saved me from stumbling. I put the stock of a nationally known company on my trial portfolio chart, simply because I had used and enjoyed the company's products. Its past record, present earnings and future prospects were unknown to me.

At the time the stock sold for 11 3/4 a share ($11.75). Each week I entered the stock's price on my chart. After six months the stock had dropped 3 1/4 points to 8 1/2. For a low-priced stock this amounted to a king-size drop, roughly 27 percent. Had I actually bought 100 shares at 11 3/4, or $1,175, and sold six months later at 8 1/2, or $850, I would have lost a whopping $325 on that amount of money.

Suppose, though, the stock had been one selling for $100 a share. A 27 percent drop in six months would mean a drop to about $73 a share, enough to start a wave of selling in the market or at least a few headaches at home.

Naturally I promptly removed the stock from my trial portfolio, thankful the deal was on paper only. To begin you will probably make mistakes, too, but it's better to stumble on paper than in the stock market with your own money.

You will be smart to settle on stocks listed on the New York Stock Exchange. I'll explain why later. For the moment it's enough for you to know that when I put the stock mentioned above, selling for 11 3/4, on my trial portfolio chart, it was not listed on the New York Stock Exchange.

RULES OF THE GAME

1. Study the stock quotations

Spread out the financial page of your daily paper to the Sales and Closing Price Quotations, or use the weekly summary of stock quotations, and do a little sleuthing. Don't let the fine print throw you. Of necessity terms and company names are abbreviated. You'll find the terms easy to figure out, and you need know the abbreviations for only the few companies you want to watch. Here's a sample stock quotation from the newspaper:

Yearly Hi	Low	Stock	Div.	Sales in 100's	Day's Hi	Lo	Close	Net Change
62-3/4	50-1/2	ATT	2.40	4189	51-7/8	51	51	-3/4

Compressed in one row of figures we find the information that American Telephone and Telegraph Company's stock sold at the highest this year for 62 3/4 ($62.75) and at the lowest for 50 1/2 ($50.50). The company pays a yearly dividend of $2.40 a share. The quotation shows that 418,900 shares were bought and sold (traded) that day. The highest price paid was 51 7/8 and the closing price was 51. The stock dropped 3/4 of a point (or 75 cents) below the closing price the day before.

Because the stock closed 7/8 of a point below its price at the opening bell of the stock market, you can assume some shareholders were more eager to sell shares that day than others were to buy. Had people clamored to buy more shares than were readily available, the price might have gone up perhaps a quarter of a point instead.

Next look up the stock quotations on each of the corporations you are considering for your portfolio. If any of them have code letters, a small letter somewhere in the quotation line for the company, refer to the explanation at the end of the quotation list. The explanation "x dividend" for x does not mean an extra dividend as one woman thought. It means that on that one particular day the stock sold for the quoted price minus the dividend. The dividend belongs to the former owner, not the new buyer. (See Chapter 4, Picking Up the Jargon.)

2. Decide on your objective

Income now? Then choose the company that pays a substantial dividend. The amount quoted is the dividend paid in one year on each share of stock. Dividends are usually distributed quarterly, though. Are you more interested in future increase in the price of your shares? Then you will probably have to forego high dividends now. But whichever you decide, be sure to look for safety of capital—high-grade stocks.

F.W. Woolworth stock selling for $29 a share, paying a dividend of $1 a share, pays a higher dividend than Honeywell, selling for $126 a share and paying $1.10 dividend.

Suppose you have about $1,000 invested in F.W. Woolworth stock at $29 a share, or 34 shares. Dividends of $1 a share a year would mean you'd get quarterly checks adding up to $34 a year.

If you put your money in Honeywell stock at $126, you would get 8 shares for around $1,000. Dividends of $1.10 on 8 shares would add up to $8.80 for the year.

Both are blue chip, high quality stocks, but one pays higher dividends than the other. This doesn't mean one is a better stock than the other, but only that one may be better suited to your purposes than the other.

3. Choose a variety of stocks

When you set up your portfolio, choose stocks in different industries. In stock jargon the word is *diversify*. More than 300 years ago George Herbert phrased the idea this way:

"The mouse that has but one hole is quickly taken." A good rule says we should invest in a number of different companies and different industries, but no more than we can conveniently watch. Professionals caution that the investor should put no more than 20 percent of her money in any one industry. When you actually buy stocks, you will probably buy stock in only one company at a time and work toward diversification.

4. Narrow your choice

From the companies you selected choose the best one in each industry, perhaps five in all. Head a page for each company, and "buy" shares totalling around $1,000 each. If one of your stocks sells for $38 a share you might buy 30 shares, while buying only 10 shares of one that sells for $93. When you really buy, of course, you have to pay the broker's commission and any tax. You also pay a higher commission when buying fewer than 100 shares of any one stock. This is called odd-lot buying since most shares sell in lots of 100 shares.

For your trial portfolio then, why not watch the stock quotations of companies whose products you use: The gasoline you buy, a paper product you use in your home, your favorite cosmetic firm, or a company home-based in your area. Do you (or your husband) work for a local branch of a national company? If so you'll have an idea whether you want to invest in its stock.

My husband counseled me to look up the earnings and price record on each stock for the past five years, including the stock's highest and lowest price for the period. You should also record the price-earnings ratio on your chart. You will find most of these statistics in Standard and Poor's *Stock Guide* or in the brokerage office. (See Chapter 3, Where to Get Help.)

Use a Trial Portfolio

Your trial portfolio chart might look something like this:

NAME OF STOCK: Top Level Company

5-year Price Range		Previous Year's Price Range		This Year's Price Range		P/E ratio	Dividend
Hi	Lo	Hi	Lo	Hi	Lo		
74	22	69	38	74	55	24	1.20

Date bought	No. shares	Price	Total cost
4/1/69	10	74	740

Six-month Price Record

Date   Closing Price

Once a week fill in the date and closing price. Add to your chart any news items about your company that you read on the business page of your daily newspaper, such as a proposed stock split, plant expansion, or new product. Watch your stocks for a period of six months. Of course six months is not long enough to judge with certainty whether a company is making or losing money for you, but that length of time will give you the feel of the market and the confidence to plunge in. You will also know whether you should weed out some of the companies you are considering. If you sit back and watch much longer you might miss out on a price rise.

When you exchange your trial portfolio for the real thing, don't destroy your trial records. Later you may want to compare figures or reconsider one of the stocks. You may also wish to use the same method later to watch other stocks you are considering.

RISK

Before reading much further you should understand that buying stocks involves a certain risk just as when a woman marries or buys a house. The woman who wants to conserve her capital needs to know there are also stocks rated as speculative in rating publications printed by brokerage houses, in Standard and Poor's *Stock Guide,* and others. So for a big choice we need to probe and ask questions and evaluate. Some people buy stocks on love-at-first-sight, or another's advice, or tips and rumors, and sometimes the stocks do turn out all right. But for the majority of us, just as in choosing a husband or a house, it pays to study the prospect, to observe it closely over a period of time.

Yet there is a difference between taking risks and gambling. Knowledge enters into taking a risk, but the woman who gambles tosses reason out the window. The one who takes a risk tries to shorten that risk, but the gambler *depends* on chance and so creates chances, trying to get something for nothing.

Merrill Lynch, Pierce, Fenner and Smith, Inc., the largest brokerage firm in the world, says an *investor* is one who takes normal risks in order to increase his capital. A *speculator* takes greater risks because he wants greater profits. He may or may not get them. But a *gambler* takes chances; he trusts to luck.

A woman can minimize the risk involved in investing by common sense and informed choice.

SOME PITFALLS THAT CAN CAUSE TROUBLE

Emotion

When you decide to buy, I hope you won't make the kind of mistake I made with the first 20 shares I bought, letting my heart, not my head, rule my choice.

At a stock seminar I had listened to the speaker cite Bethlehem Steel's stock as a good income producer over the past years. It was the Christmas season and I thought how appropriate to buy 20 shares of Bethlehem Steel. No man would understand such reasoning, nor do I now. It was a good stock, and still is, but I had not investigated it, nor compared prices over a period of time, or I would have known that the stock sold at an all-time high right then. Soon after I bought, it began to drop and never did go back to the high price I paid. Emotions will get you nowhere in the stock market.

Popularity

The market's most popular stock is not always a good investment for a beginner. The stock's very popularity may have run up the price so that it's not a good buy at the time. The New York Stock Exchange publishes a daily list of 15 or 20 stocks most heavily traded. Some of these stocks rise, some fall in price, each day. Yet their popularity alone does not mean these stocks are good values for the woman who wants to protect her capital and see it grow.

Tips and free advice

When anyone wants to tip you off to a good value or a sure winner, don't swallow the lure until you investigate.

Here's an interesting but sad sidelight on "hot" tips. The Muldoons (not their real name) learned the hard way that tips can be hot enough to burn. In their suburb lived an auto and casualty insurance salesman. He and his family spent money much more freely than anyone else there. When the Muldoons' daughter got one cashmere sweater, the insurance man's daughter got six. When the Muldoons' two little boys played in their back yard with a sand box, the other family's children spun around in a pint-sized merry-go-round, complete with music. The rest of the neighbors couldn't help but see the expensive cars and trips the insurance man's family enjoyed.

One day he talked to the Muldoons about an auto and casualty insurance company he was forming. He painted a fantastic picture of future gains. Other neighbors joined in with him to form a partnership.

"You want to get in on the ground floor," he told the Muldoons. "I'm selling shares of stock, but it won't be for long. A hundred shares today will put your two little boys through college." He also explained there would be no dividends, because he'd put all the profits back into the company for future growth.

To the Muldoons the venture sounded like easy money. They put in $2,000 and sat back to wait for their shares to increase. Nothing much happened to the shares. The Muldoons still have them in their safety box. What did happen was that the high-spending insurance neighbor started spending money that wasn't his. The other partners ousted him. Today the stock has absolutely no resale value.

Perhaps you wonder how the Muldoons could be taken in. Remember, the man who sold them the stock was a close neighbor, apparently making money, a successful businessman.

A woman must learn to turn a deaf ear to "hot" tips from anyone unless she's sure the informer knows his way around in the stock market or has investigated a particular stock.

In contrast, I felt justified in giving advice not long ago when a young man asked me for suggestions. He had $2,000 he was eager to spend on stock. Because I had lately investigated them, I suggested he buy Sears Roebuck stock and Dayton's. In a short time he got in on price increases on both stocks and a stock split on one. The stocks were good values at the time.

WHAT A BEGINNER CAN EXPECT

When a woman buys stocks she hands over money, hard-earned, hard-saved or gift-easy, for a paper certificate. You expect this money back at a later date, and because you have not had the use of your money, you expect interest too. But most important, you want your money to buy just as much for you then as if you had spent it right now for a fur coat or a car. If it does not, you may not have taken the best care of what has come into your hands.

For this reason a sharp-witted woman will consider good growth stocks as part of her portfolio. If a stock never increases in value, or even drops, it is the same as fixed dollars in the bank. On the other hand, growth stocks, which defer present income by not paying high dividends, usually increase or appreciate in value. The company turns back (or plows, as the professionals say) its earnings into the company for research, new product development, new equipment, and other expansion. All this increases the value of the stock and the price tends to rise. One clue to selecting a growth stock is the extent of the company's past history of growth. Many young companies also have good prospects for growth, as we shall see in a later chapter.

PROFIT MARGIN

A term to begin to understand is *high profit margin.* Tuck it in the back of your mind for the present. You will find it cropping up repeatedly as you read about the stock market. Profit margin is simply the amount the company earns on each share of its stock. High profit margins allow the company to put profits back into its business, thus financing its own expansion instead of renting money from outside sources.

Also watch for management that is imaginative and research-minded. (See Chapter 8, How to Evaluate a Company.)

SAMPLE TRIAL PORTFOLIO

When I made up my hypothetical portfolio I chose a firm that deals in hospital supplies and a variety of other items, an oil company, an airline, a cosmetic firm, and a food corporation. Here's the record:

	1965			1968		
Stock	No. shares bought	Price (round numbers)	Cost	No. shares owned	Price (round numbers)	Value
Avon Prod.	20	61	$1,220	20	112	$2,240
General Foods	10	82	820	10	66	660
Johnson and Johnson	10	117	1,170	30 (3 for 1 split)	76	2,280
Standard Oil N.J.	10	87	870	10	67	670
Northwest Airlines	10	78	780	20 (2 for 1 split)	67	1,340
		Total	$4,860			$7,190
		Gain				2,330

The figures show about a 47 percent increase in value of the shares in about three years, not counting dividends. Nice to think about in retrospect. Sad I didn't actually buy one or two of those stocks in 1965. Some, of course, show bigger gains than others. Still my hypothetical portfolio stands as an example of how a modest amount of capital, carefully invested in sound companies and held for a few years, even through the market crunch of 1966, can work for you.

Once you become a stockholder, make-believe or real, you should pick up news items about your companies from the business page of the newspaper. When you really own stock the company will automatically mail its quarterly and annual reports to you. You'll learn a lot about a company by careful study of its annual report.

Use a Trial Portfolio

The more you know about investing in stocks and the company you invest in before you actually buy, the more confidence you will have. It is to your advantage to be informed.

I remember ruefully the time I went to our broker (or account executive as he is called) to buy my first $1,000 worth of stock on my own. I said I wanted the shares in my own name, but when the confirmation slip came, the account remained in my husband's name. I had not made it clear that I wanted to open my own account.

To begin investing you need money, although not a fortune, but also important, you need know-how, the more the better. Even if you're not ready to spend your money on stocks now, you can prepare for the time when you will invest by setting up a trial portfolio.

To Benefit Most from This Chapter:

1. Set up a hypothetical portfolio of stocks for about five companies in as many different industries. "Buy" about $1,000 worth of each stock. Follow the sample chart earlier in this chapter.
2. Write to each company you select for your trial portfolio asking for a copy of its latest annual report.

Where to Get Help   3

When you hire a cateress you pay for her knowledge and experience as well as her products. If you use the services of an interior decorator you pay for his knowledge, his search for the right picture, fabric, or carpet. When you take your car to the garage to find out what rattles under the hood, you pay for the serviceman's know-how. So in the world of investing you can call on professionals—investment counselors, investment services, investment funds, and mutual funds. They'll make all the decisions for you, usually with satisfactory results, but you pay for such knowledge and service.

You can learn to manage and increase your money. By taking advantage of free and inexpensive helps, you can develop into a capable do-it-yourselfer. Why not put yourself in charge?

Like any new skill or knowledge, though, this requires study and careful application of principles learned. Time spent each day for six months or so reading and researching the field of investments will produce a solid background on which to build. By continuing to build on this knowledge and constantly studying, you will be capable of managing and increasing not only the money you have today but the money of a lifetime. Experts tell us a working gal's lifetime pay checks may add up to $200,000 or even more—a hefty sum funneled into a woman's hands.

LEARN TO STUDY

Before tackling your own investment problems, determine to spend an hour or two a day studying. Any college or adult education course requires this minimum of study time. After you finish your apprenticeship you can cut down on time if you wish. But don't be surprised if you find your interest in the subject compounded.

Take a tip from college students who depend on a few tricks to help them study. Perhaps you have forgotten or have never heard of a quick and efficient way to read a book for a learning experience. Here is one:

Scan the Index for chapter headings.

Read the Preface or Forward or Note from the Author.

Ask yourself: What do I expect to learn by reading this book? This chapter?

Look for the topic sentence of each paragraph. Most non-fiction paragraphs contain a topic sentence, one that explains what the paragraph means. The rest of the paragraph amplifies the topic sentence. Sometimes the topic sentence is the first one, sometimes the last. It may even show up somewhere in between. When you discover the topic sentence, underline it. Think about it a moment before reading the next paragraph.

Reread all your underlined sentences before going on to the next chapter. If you have questions, read the paragraph again.

Apply or test what you have learned. Of course, you can read straight through any book and pick up ideas and methods that will help you. But you will benefit most by taking each chapter slowly and following any suggestions at the end of each chapter.

SPECIAL HELPS

Next take advantage of as many of the following as possible.

1. Grade school math

Review what you learned in grade school about percentage. Do you remember how to solve these three problems?

        9 is ____ percent of 81?
        ____ is 9 percent of 81?
        9 is 9 percent of ____ ?

Figuring percentages is a tool you'll use again and again as you manage your money.

2. Daily newspaper

Look for news items on the stocks you chose for your hypothetical portfolio. You may learn that the airline you selected ran into labor problems last week. This will probably cause a drop in income and your stock may decrease in price. In contrast the news that another airline is branching out into the airlift business can cause that company's stock to spiral.

When I set up my hypothetical portfolio authorities had just approved Johnson and Johnson's new birth control pill for release to the public. At the same time Protestants, Catholics, and the government, shuddering at the population explosion, began to rethink their stand in this area. I put Johnson and Johnson in my "portfolio" at 117 5/8 a share. Three years later the stock was worth more than twice that amount, largely because of demand for a new product much publicized in the newspapers.

3. The Wall Street Journal

Printed Monday through Friday, *The Wall Street Journal* carries few recipes, fashion, or supermarket ads, and it costs $28 a year. Chiefly, it prints articles and editorials on American corporations, their officers and directors, and the economy. It carries complete records of stock transactions on the New York and American Stock Exchange. It lists the bid and asked prices of over-the-counter stocks, investment and mutual funds, gives stock averages, and various other market information.

4. Barron's

A weekly paper that costs $18 a year, *Barron's* contains fine statistical coverage of all phases of the stock market, as well as informative articles on corporations and investing.

5. Stock averages

Dow Jones and Company began publishing a daily stock price average more than 70 years ago. First came the Dow Jones industrial average, which now consists of 30 firms. Later the compilers added the averages for 20 railroads and later still for 15 public utilities. These averages, comprised of top-grade stocks, reflect, in the opinion of those who compile them, the general market behavior. Statisticians compute the Dow Jones industrial average hourly by adding up the price of one share of each of the 30 industrials and dividing by an adjusted divisor. When one of the stocks splits or distributes a stock dividend, the divisor changes. Every Monday *The Wall Street Journal* lists the names of the stocks comprising the averages (the same ones for some time now) and also the current divisor (2.011 at the end of 1968).

When people say, "The market dropped four points today," or "The Dow Jones went up three points," they generally mean the Dow Jones industrial average. You will see it flashed on TV screens, on the electric sign outside some banks and brokerage houses. In 1968 the Dow Jones industrial average fluctuated between a low of 825.13 and a high of 985.21. In 1932, during the depression, the average reached a low of 40.46. In February 1966 the Dow hit an all-time high of 995.15.

Some investors put more faith in other averages, or indexes, such as the New York Stock Exchange's average of

60 stocks, or Standard and Poor's 500-stock composite, compiled on an hourly basis. The American Stock Exchange also compiles an average. Though some experts consider these more accurate indicators of the market's trend, the spell of the old and familiar clings to the Dow Jones industrial average, the one most investors check.

6. The Exchange Magazine (Dept. IF, 11 Wall St., New York)

A pocket magazine published monthly by the New York Stock Exchange for $2.50 a year, *The Exchange Magazine* contains information on investing and the economy.

7. Standard and Poor's Stock Guide

Issued monthly, the *Stock Guide* not only rates nearly 5,000 companies (A, B, C, etc.) but gives a wealth of statistics on them.

8. Magazines

Business Week, Time, U.S. News and World Report devote sections to American business, the economy, and the stock market. Other investment and business magazines, *Financial World, Forbes, Fortune,* print sketches on top management, and even recommend stocks to buy or sell. *Forbes* publishes an annual report and rates 500 American corporations. *Financial World* puts out a 12-year stock record you should own. Women's magazines also occasionally print helpful articles on the subject of investing.

9. Investment seminars

Watch the papers for advertisements of stock seminars for women. Or possibly your bank will notify you when it holds one. Arranged by brokerage houses and banks, often in cooperation with a department store, such seminars provide a good introduction to the subject of investments. Experienced

Where to Get Help

and trained men from the brokerage office or bank, from the faculty of a university or business school lecture on the stock market and the theory of investing. Not long ago I listened to a charming and informed young woman from Paine, Webber, Jackson and Curtis talk on the subject. Perhaps you will see a short movie in color depicting the stock market through the eyes of a woman buying her first shares of stock.

10. Newsletters, investment services and charts

Barron's, Research Institute Investors Service, Kiplinger's Washington Letter, to name a few, are all rather costly and not primarily intended for the small investor. You should, however, be aware of them.

11. Classes and correspondence courses

These are offered by various financial firms. Ads for them appear in magazines and newspapers. If you can spare the time an adult course in investments and one in economics will be of great help.

12. Investment clubs

A lot of women learn about investing by joining or starting an investment club. About a dozen members, friends, or people with a common interest in investing meet once a month and put in $10 or more each. After study of various stocks the group votes on the shares it buys or sells. An investment club conducts its business with just one broker. Clubs made up of women have a good record. (See Chapter 7, What You Can Learn from Investment Clubs.)

13. Business section of the public library

The beginner, who probably won't want to spend a great deal on such helps at first, will find most of them in the library. Here you can scan copies of *The Wall Street Journal*,

Barron's, Reader's Guide to Periodical Literature and read current articles. Also check the card index file for recent books on the subject. (See the Bibliography at end of this book.)

14. TV programs

For some time recently, educational TV, KTCA, Minneapolis presented "This Week on Wall Street." A broker-reporter team reviewed market activity for the week, pointed out business news and trends, and held an interview with a corporation executive or economics authority.

In Los Angeles, "The Station That Means Business" ran for a time an investment program against a background of stock quotations. A stockbroker answered telephone queries and talked about the market.

Other stations across the country have picked up the idea.

15. Reliable friend

Do you know a man or woman who has capably managed his own capital, someone who will spend a little time helping you get your feet wet? What about your attorney, banker, accountant, or a business acquaintance? Can any of these steer you to a reliable broker?

16. Brokerage house

Perhaps you will get the most help here, for the brokerage house, eager for business, is more than willing to supply you with a pile of free information, such as printed reports on any corporation that interests you. These reports include the company's assets, liabilities, and prospects for growth or increased earnings. The broker also offers free booklets on understanding the stock market and the language of investing.

Where to Get Help

One broker even gave a series of lectures on investing, on closed circuit, to prisoners in Michigan. Other brokers give investment courses to beginners, charging a small fee.

The New York office of most brokerage firms maintains a staff of men with degrees in chemistry, electronics, engineering, and other subjects for the purpose of survey, research and analysis of corporations. They will analyze your portfolio (the real one) periodically and suggest ways to better it through buying new stocks or selling poor ones.

Despite all this free help and advice, remember it's your money. Before you buy a stock, find out what's in the package.

VISIT A BROKERAGE OFFICE

When you visit a brokerage office, choose a member of the New York Stock Exchange. Their offices are located in hundreds of cities and smaller towns, in Grand Central Station, city department stores, and shopping centers. They really want to sell you. If you live in a very small town, you may have to travel to a nearby large city. Although your banker can handle stock transactions for you, don't skip visiting a brokerage office.

Tell the information girl you want to watch the electric board of stock quotations. Ask for a guide to the symbols used for stocks, or at least the stocks you are watching. For example, the code for General Motors is GM, Control Data is CD, American Telephone and Telegraph Company is T, and so forth.

At this time you may or may not ask for the help of an account executive (the man who will help you when you actually buy and sell stocks). You might explain that you want to invest some time in the future and would like to get acquainted with the electronic board. After sitting in one of the chairs provided and watching the symbols sprint across the board, you will sense the expectancy, the urgency, and the busyness of the brokerage office.

An account executive finds plenty to keep him busy even though you see him reclining in a swivel chair, smoking a pipe, and staring into space. He watches the board, decides which ones of his hundreds of customers will be interested in a good buy or adverse turn of events. One day he will pick up the phone in answer to your call, touch the button on the quote machine on his desk, and tell you instantly, for example, not only what Standard Oil of California is selling for at the moment, but a dozen other pertinent facts about the stock.

When you do introduce yourself to this man (or woman), remember he deals constantly in quick decisions and so has little time to philosophize or teach on the job. Be clear in your mind about your questions before you talk to him. After you open your account and become acquainted with the office, deal as much as possible with him over the phone.

AMOUNT INVESTED

Are you wondering whether the amount you want to invest is too small for a broker to bother with? If you have less than $500, which would buy 10 shares of any one of a number of high-grade stocks, you might consider the New York Stock Exchange Monthly Investment Plan. A type of installment buying, this plan allows you to pay as little as $40 a quarter. Your payment buys fractional shares of whatever stock you choose. The brokerage firm credits the shares and dividends to your account. Commissions are somewhat higher proportionately than on direct sales. The Monthly Investment Plan pushes the woman who needs a definite commitment into saving regularly. But for the more disciplined woman, it might be wiser to bank the money, collect interest, until you have $500 or so, and then buy your own shares.

Even if you have $5,000 to invest you will be wiser not to put it all in one stock, but to choose four or five different corporations and buy them at different times throughout the year. Your investment then buys shares in several different industries, some at a time during the year when the stock might sell for less than at another time. Ben Franklin called this putting your eggs in more than one basket. Brokers use the term *diversify*.

INTUITION, SENTIMENT AND "HOT" TIPS

Are we forgetting something? Like woman's intuition? Emotion, sentiment, and friendly tips? Well and good, if so. Still a word or two about these obstacles to sensible investing may prove helpful. A woman's intuition can sometimes steer her out of a bad deal or head her toward a profitable one. But emotion and sentiment are out of place in investing. I had to have this pointed out to me.

My husband's estate included 100 shares of blue chip stock, bought years ago, the first shares he had ever owned. Several times my broker said, "You ought to sell that stock. Earnings are down and management is ultra-conservative."

Recalling how thrilled we were when we could afford to buy the stock, and also thinking of that long thin envelope that came every three months—the dividend check—I said, "I'll think about it. But I have a sentimental attachment to that stock."

"Hang sentiment!" the broker exploded and swiveled in his chair. "Here," he said. "Read these reports on companies with good prospects."

Chuckling at his getting overheated about my $2,000 worth of stock, I went home to check my records. I found that the stock was worth less than my husband had paid for it, that it had been on a slide for some time. The next day I phoned the broker, "Sell!"

The broker-recommended shares I bought in their place increased 50 percent in a year's time, or $1,000.

And "hot" tips! From your hairdresser's husband, the fellow at work who speculates in dollar stocks, the coffee party hostess whose best friend's aunt plays the stock market and made $10,000 in Zerox—or Kleenex—or something with an "x" in it. Forget it. The only basis for a woman's buying shares of stock is informed selection, either by experts—or herself.

Does all this sound like work? It is. If you received an inheritance of $35,000 tomorrow, would you go out and spend it as fast as you could without thought of what the interest on that much money could do for you for the rest of your life? Would you let it streak through your fingers without once trying to protect it, let alone increase it?

I am reminded of my friend Irma who told me after her husband's death, "If I could sit down and talk to Norm about our finances, I'd ask him why he didn't let me in on the facts of the hard, practical business world. I wish he'd talked to me about taxes and fraud, and how to figure true interest on installment buying. I wish he'd shown me how much capital a woman needs to get even a small quarterly interest payment."

Well, Irma or anyone else in her fix can do something about it all. Not all of us receive large inheritances, though almost every married woman can expect some day to be left in charge of her husband's estate. During a lifetime a woman finds thousands and thousands of dollars skimming through her hands. Higher incomes abound, but statisticians tell us it takes $14,000 annual income today for a family of four to live on the same standard a salary of $5,000 provided in 1938. A woman's money needs protection. It also needs to increase with the cost of living. By study and wise decisions you can protect and increase your capital.

The Queen of England once said to Fritz Kreisler, world renowned violinist, "Ah, you play with such ease. It looks all pleasure when you play the violin."

Where to Get Help

"Your Majesty," said Kreisler, "to play the violin is indeed a great pleasure, but first I was a *drudge.*"

To Benefit Most from This Chapter:

1. Make room at your desk or the kitchen table to spread out papers, pamphlets, magazines, and books.
2. Start a file in a carton, large enough to hold manila file folders upright. Label a folder for each company you are watching. Put in the folder any news report or other information you read or hear on the air about that company.
3. Start a clipping file of stock columns and stock articles. Identify these by date and name of the paper or magazine.
4. Buy and read a current copy of *The Wall Street Journal.* Keep it for future reference.
5. Buy and read a current copy of a financial magazine.
6. Visit a brokerage office and watch the electronic board. Where are the Dow Jones averages posted? Is the DJ industrial average up or down from yesterday's average?

Picking Up the Jargon   4

Any new skill, interest, or knowledge requires attention to special language, or jargon, used by the experts. Teachers talk about under-achievers and controlled vocabulary. Preachers expound on eschatology and ecumenicalism. Fans of football, racing cars, space, all speak a lingo of their own.

Similarly the stock market employs its own words and terms. Some are rather empty phrases, such as "buying on balance," "overbought," and "oversold." Others are handy tools a woman investor needs to understand and use. Here are the terms I found most puzzling as a beginner:

ACCOUNT EXECUTIVE

The salesman or woman you deal with at the brokerage office. He opens your account, recommends sound stocks, buys or sells shares for you, charges you a commission, set by regulation. He needs to know about your goals, whether long-term growth of capital, fairly high income, or a lesser combination. He is essentially a salesman, usually keen and knowledgeable about his wares. Because he represents his firm, the actual broker, you will probably refer to him as your broker.

ASSETS

The value of everything a corporation owns. Also what others owe the company.

AVERAGES AND INDEXES

Barometers to show whether the stock market is higher or lower than previously. The Dow Jones averages remain the oldest and most popular measures of stock activity. In 1896 Charles Dow compiled a daily average of 12 selected high-grade industrial stocks. In 1928 the list increased to 30 firms. In 1897 he published a railroad average of 20 stocks. In 1929 the Dow Jones Company added a public utilities average of 15 stocks. The company also compiles an average of all three of the above, and other averages.

Each day as soon as the New York Stock Exchange opens at 10:00 a.m., and every hour until it closes, Dow Jones statisticians read the stock ticker for the latest price of each of the stocks comprising the average. Then they add and divide by an adjusted divisor, which takes into account stock splits, stock dividends, and other changes. The average goes by Teletype to branch offices across the country.

Another average, Standard and Poor's 500-stock composite, represents 90 percent of the market value of all stocks listed on the New York Stock Exchange—425 industrials, 25 railroads, and 50 utilities, including 62 of the stocks used in the Dow Jones averages.

Other averages are: New York Stock Exchange's composite, American Stock Exchange's comprehensive index, the National Quotation Bureau's industrial average of 35 over-the-counter stocks, the Associated Press average.

AVERAGING UP

Buying more of a stock as its price goes up, while averaging down means making additional purchases of a stock as its price drops.

BEAR MARKET

When the value of stocks on the market falls for a period of time.

BID AND ASKED

Bid is the highest price anyone has offered to pay for a stock at a given time. Asked is the lowest price anyone will sell for at that time. In the case of mutual funds, the higher asked price includes the salesman's commission and other costs.

BIG BOARD

Name for the New York Stock Exchange because it lists more stocks on its electric board and more stocks trade there than on any other exchange.

BLUE CHIPS

Common stock of any well-known, usually large, established company with good earnings and regular dividends paid over a long period of time. In other words, a leader in its industry.

BOND

A promise to repay the amount borrowed sometime in the future. The time of repayment, anywhere from five to thirty years, is called the maturity date. A bondholder is a creditor of a company, not a part owner as a stockholder is. When anyone buys bonds he lends his money to a company or the government at a determined rate of interest paid semi-annually. If a company fails, the bondholder gets his money before the stockholder gets a dollar. For this reason investors consider bonds a safe type of security. (Yet there are speculative bonds.) United States government bonds rate as the safest investment because the government stands behind the promise to pay. During inflation, though, bonds rate with savings accounts and other conservative fixed income.

Bonds are usually issued for $1,000 or multiples of that amount. A stock quotation for a bond may be confusing at first since the last digit of the price is dropped. A bond quoted as selling for 96.51 means the bond sells for $965.10.

BOOK VALUE

Also termed net asset value, the book value means the net assets that back up the common stock. To arrive at book value you add the amount of total liabilities and the amount required to liquidate any preferred stock, and deduct this amount from total assets. Then divide the result by the number of shares of common stock outstanding.

Although book value becomes meaningful when a company liquidates, it should not be used when considering market value of a stock.

BROKER

Though the brokerage firm who paid for a seat on the national exchange is the real broker, usage hands this title to the salesman you deal with in the local brokerage office, the account executive.

BROKER'S COMMISSION

Minimum commission rates, per share:

ROUND LOTS (100 shares or more)

Under $100	As mutually agreed
$ 100 to $ 399	2 percent plus $1
400 to 2,399	1 percent plus $5
2,400 to 4,999	1/2 percent plus $17
5,000 and over	1/10 percent plus $37

ODD LOTS (less than 100 shares)

Under $100	As mutually agreed
$ 100 to $ 399	2 percent plus $3
400 to 2,399	1 percent plus $7
2,400 to 4,999	1/2 percent plus $19
5,000 and over	1/10 percent plus $39

BULL MARKET

When the value of stocks rises for a period of time.

CAPITAL GAIN OR CAPITAL LOSS

What anyone gains or loses in the sale of property over the original cost. A short-term capital gain or loss is property sold six months or less from the date of purchase. A short-term capital gain is taxed as regular income on a tax return. A long-term capital gain is one held more than six months. Only half the gain is taxed.

CERTIFICATE

Evidence of share ownership. Engraved with a variety of symbols and legendary characters, the crisp 8" x 12" time-honored stock certificate now stands in a spot marked "guilty." With the huge increase of volume on the stock market, experts point to the stock certificate as causing unnecessary record-keeping, as being outmoded. At work on a computerized system, authorities hope to come up with a better system. Perhaps in the not too distant future a punched card and a printed notice will take the place of the certificate.

COMMON STOCK

When a company files papers for incorporation, it indicates the number of shares of common stock it will offer for sale to the public. A corporation sells shares of common stock in order to finance its business, expand it, or conduct research. All shareholders own the corporation in common. When you buy 100 shares of American Can Company common stock, you own the company in common with 17,655,616 (1967) shareholders. So your personal ownership is nebulous. Naturally all the 17 million stockholders want their company to prosper, their stock to increase in value, their dividends to go up. Through their combined strength shareholders do have something to say about how the company operates.

COMPOUND INTEREST

Interest figured on an original principal, plus on interest as it accumulates.

Picking Up the Jargon

CONGLOMERATES

A corporation that makes a habit of buying up smaller companies. The difference between conglomerates and ordinary mergers is that mergers buy smaller companies as an outlet for their products, or to absorb a competitor, or to diversify in related fields. An example of a merger is Ford Motor Company and Philco Radio. Conglomerates, on the other hand, buy up other companies in unrelated lines of business, such as Litton Industries, shipbuilders and Royal Typewriter Company.

CONTRACTUAL PLAN

Used by mutual funds, a long-term contract for buying shares regularly. The bulk of the salesman's commission comes out of early payment, thus penalizing the buyer if she drops out early in the plan.

COST BASE OR BASIS

What you paid for the stock, including the broker's commission. Divide this amount by the number of shares you buy. Figure your cost base separately for each block of shares. Should you exercise rights and later want to sell shares, consult a tax expert for advice on how to figure the cost base.

If you receive the stock as an inheritance, your cost base is the price per share on the date of death of the owner. (In some cases, one year from the date of death. Check with an attorney.)

When you receive shares as an outright gift, your cost base is the same as the donor's.

A stock split does not change your actual cost base. You have twice as many shares, each costing half as much as before.

An accurate cost base becomes important when you want to sell the stock and figure your capital gain or loss.

CYCLICAL STOCK

Stock of a company whose earnings tend to run in cycles. Examples: Toy stocks usually go up after the big sales at Christmas, and farm machinery stocks rise after a good spring season.

DEBENTURE

Issued today by many companies in place of bonds. The owner of a debenture, like a bondowner, is a creditor of the company. On the minus side, the debenture holder does not own a part of the company. He cannot vote on company business, nor does the size of his debenture or any interest paid increase with increased company profits.

On the plus side the debenture owner will find his interest paid before common stock dividends. Should the company fail, debenture holders must be paid off before common stockholders.

DEFLATION

A tightening of available money and credit, so that the country produces more goods and services than people are able or willing to buy. This sends prices down, which in turn reduces the number of employees needed, wages paid, resulting in even less buying power.

DIVERSIFY

Dividing investment money among different types of securities—preferred stocks, common stocks, bonds—and among several different industries instead of putting it all into one company. Shrewd investors also diversify their common stocks by holding a mixture of blue chips, glamor, and speculative stocks. *Warning:* Avoid choosing more companies than you can watch carefully.

DOLLAR-COST AVERAGING

To invest a fixed amount at fixed intervals, say $100 a

month or $500 twice a year, in specific stocks. You buy the number of shares at the time that cost a sum nearest your fixed amount. Naturally you buy more shares when the price is low than when it is high.

A variation of this is to buy a fixed number of shares at fixed times, say 20 shares twice a year. You probably will pay less for 20 shares at some times than others. To come out ahead on this, though, you must be sure to sell at a price higher than the average price you paid for all shares.

DOLLAR STOCKS (Sometimes called penny stocks)

Low-priced, highly speculative issues selling for less than $10 a share. For some reason the aura of a bargain hangs around such stocks. The theory persists that 100 shares of a $2.00 stock cost only $200, and if it goes up to $5 a share — yes, yes. Occasionally this happens, but time after time the the risks are too great and the money vanishes.

ECONOMY

The circular flow of a nation's needs and demands and the money spent for these, plus its labors and skills that produce goods and services, paid for in wages and salaries.

EX-DIVIDEND

Indicated as "x" in the stock quotation just before the number of shares traded for a particular company, meaning that this day the stock is selling without dividend. Anyone buying that stock on that day will not receive the dividend to be paid by the company in about three weeks. The dividend will go to the previous owner.

Here's why. The directors of a corporation vote to declare a quarterly dividend of perhaps 50 cents a share on June 1. In order to give themselves, or the transfer agent, time to verify the names of their thousands of stockholders, and make out the dividend checks, the "record" or cut-off date is also announced, perhaps as May 10. To receive the June 1 dividend a stockholder must be recorded on the company's books before the cut-off date. Then in order to give the brokerage house time to complete sales on that particular stock, five days are subtracted from the record date. So that to be a stockholder of record and receive the dividend to be paid June 1, you would have to own the stock at least on May 5. Anyone who bought shares on or after May 6 would not receive the June 1 dividend.

On the ex-dividend date the amount of the dividend is subtracted from the quoted price of the stock. If the stock sells for $75 and the company declares a quarterly dividend of 50 cents, the stock would be quoted as 74½ on the ex-dividend day.

EX-RIGHTS

When a company offers additional shares for sale, it may first offer rights to buy these shares at a reduced rate for a limited time to its shareholders. Only those shareholders who own stock before a certain cut-off date, the date of offering the rights, will appear on the company books. But in order to have time for office work, an additional five days is subtracted from this date. Anyone who buys after that time is not eligible to exercise the rights. On the ex-rights day, the value of one right is deducted from the price of the share.

GLAMOR STOCK

A stock with a glamorous new process or invention or some other factor that focuses the investment spotlight on the company and gives its stock a position of glamor. This pushes up the price so that the price-earnings ratio is disproportionately high.

GROSS NATIONAL PRODUCT (GNP)

The best measure of our nation's economy, the market value of all goods and services produced in this country in a single year. GNP has increased an average of 3 percent a year since 1900.

GROWTH STOCKS

Show a consistent rise in value. If they do go down, each dip is less than the time before and the growth is steadily upward. Sales and earnings grow faster than the economy as a whole. Some may not pay dividends, preferring to put the money earned back into the company. Other companies pay dividends, which, while often low, do increase over the years. Growth stocks have the ability to substantially increase sales and earnings over the years above other companies.

INCOME STOCKS

Pay high dividends regularly, but the actual price of the stock is apt to remain fairly stable.

INFLATION

Increase in prices resulting from greater demand than supply of goods and services. Present-day economists claim that if we want a high rate of employment and economic growth in our country, we must accept a certain degree of inflation.

INSTITUTIONS

Large investors, including investment trusts and mutual funds, pension and profit-sharing funds, insurance companies, colleges and universities, private investment funds, and trusts of large estates.

INVESTMENT FUNDS AND TRUSTS

See Chapter 10, What You Should Know About Trusts and Mutual Funds.

LEVERAGE

Consists of preferred stocks and bonds, other loans and

debts used by a corporation to acquire added capital. With more capital the company can expand. When interest is low and yield high, the result is rapid income growth. But this leverage can have a depressing effect on a corporation's common stock. In times of depression it can wipe out the profits. In a decline in a company's business, high leverage can work against its common stock, since preferred stock dividends and bond interest must be paid first.

LIABILITIES

Everything a company owes or is liable for.

LIQUIDITY

Capable of quick sale.

LISTED STOCKS

Stocks listed on a national stock exchange. To have its stock so listed a corporation must pass rigid specifications and abide by certain rules laid down by the Securities and Exchange Commission. Many corporations attain national prestige and increased sales by passing these requirements and "going public." Other high-grade companies, perhaps regional in nature, prefer to remain unlisted. Banks, insurance companies, government and corporation bonds trade unlisted.

MARGIN

Buying listed stocks by making a down payment on the full amount of the stock, borrowing the rest at interest from the brokerage firm. Investors or speculators buy stocks on margin with the hope that the stock will go up enough to cover the amount borrowed. Should the stock sink instead of rise in a certain length of time, the broker will phone the borrower to cover losses, or pay more money. There is nothing immoral about buying on margin. It's a sort of installment buying, but not for the beginner. If the market tumbles, you stand to lose. To buy on margin you must have a minimum of $2,000 to pay on the stock. There is also a set

Picking Up the Jargon

limit on the amount of stock a customer can buy on margin. At present the rate is 80 percent, the amount the customer must advance, and 20 percent the amount she can borrow.

MARKET PRICE

Sometimes termed "at the market." This is the current price for which a stock or other security sells.

MONTHLY INVESTMENT PLAN (MIP)

Whereby an investor may acquire shares listed on the New York Stock Exchange for as little as $40 a month or $40 a quarter, plus the customary commission. Regular payments buy shares or fractional shares of any stock selected, with the advantage of dollar-cost averaging.

MUTUAL FUNDS

See Chapters 10 and 11.

NATIONAL ASSOCIATION OF SECURITIES DEALERS, INC. (NASD)

Brokers and dealers who police and regulate the over-the-counter market.

NET ASSET VALUE

Used primarily by investment trusts and mutual funds to determine the value of their shares. The fund figures this twice daily by deducting its liabilities from its assets, then dividing the balance by the number of shares outstanding. The net asset value of a share is the amount an open-end fund will pay for its shares.

NET CHANGE

On the day's quotation means change from the previous day's close, not the change for the day. What makes the opening price one day different from the closing price of the previous day? For one, a pileup of buy or sell orders received in a branch office after the New York Stock exchange closed.

An international ruckus or a national disaster can also influence the opening price and what buyers will pay.

ODD LOTS

Generally stocks trade on the market in round lots of 100 shares, or in the case of certain stocks 10, 25, or 50 shares. But many shareholders trade fewer shares—10, 20, 30, or even one or two shares of a high-priced stock such as IBM. For odd-lot sales the broker calls on an odd-lot dealer to complete the buy or sell order, charging an additional odd-lot commission. At present the commission is 12½ cents a share on stocks below $55 and 25 cents a share on stocks above $55.

OVER-THE-COUNTER MARKET

Not a central market place, but a vast coast-to-coast network of dealers, connected by phone, Teletype, and electronic quote machines. The market's main hub lies in New York City. There is no counter, though at one time over-the-counter stocks (OTC) traded across the counter of a bank. Neither does the OTC market have a public ticker service or quotation board. (Plans for such are in the offing.) Instead quotations are distributed by Teletype to brokers and dealers.

Although OTC dealers must register with the Securities and Exchange Commission, OTC stocks are not subject to the same strict regulations as listed stocks. They are, however, subject to the ethical regulations of the National Association of Securities Dealers. This association issues daily reports for over 1,500 OTC stocks, printing a sampling in large city papers. The report shows not actual trades but the bid and asked prices.

Approximately 30,000 unlisted stocks comprise the OTC market. These stocks range from highly speculative "dollar"

Picking Up the Jargon

stocks to high-grade government and corporation bonds, bank and insurance stocks, some public utilities, and many foreign companies. A number of listed stocks are, on occasion, traded over-the-counter.

The broker who represents you negotiates or bargains for the price with one or more dealers instead of the auction system as in the case of listed stocks.

Any company desiring to offer shares of stock for public sale must first submit to selling them over-the-counter. Some companies later meet the stiff standards of the stock exchanges (such as amount of assets and annual earnings and ratio of outstanding shares to stockholders) and may then be listed on a national stock exchange. Others trade over-the-counter indefinitely. Despite many high-grade issues, OTC stocks are, on the whole, more speculative than listed stocks.

PAPER PROFITS

The profit you would make if you sold your shares today at the market price. (Don't forget to subtract income tax for capital gains!)

PAR

Because the term "par value" is generally misunderstood and has lost its significance, many companies set a very low par value, $1 or $5, on a share of their stock. Some corporations do not attach any par or stated value to their stock. But in the case of preferred stock or bonds, par can be important. Should the company fail, and money were available, preferred stockholders and bondholders would be paid the par value of their shares.

PARTICIPATING PREFERRED STOCK

Preferred stock which permits the holder, under certain conditions, to share with common stockholders in increased earnings, either by increased dividends or value of the stock.

PERFORMANCE

The rise and fall in value of a stock, the company's income, assets, and earnings compared with the market as a whole.

PORTFOLIO

The securities held by an investor.

PREFERRED STOCK

In some ways preferred stock takes precedence over the common stock. The company must pay dividends on its preferred stock before paying dividends on its common stock. Should disaster overtake the corporation, preferred stockholders receive payment for their shares before any common stockholder. But preferred stockholders usually do not have the right to vote on company plans.

PRICE-EARNINGS RATIO (P/E)

The ratio between the current market price of a stock and its annual earnings (not dividends) per share. That is, the current market price of a share of stock divided by the year's earnings per share equals the price-earnings ratio. If a stock sells at $60, reports yearly earnings of $2.50 per share, dividing the price of the stock by the earnings gives a P/E ratio of 24 to 1. The stock then sells for 24 times its earnings.

Growth stocks often have high P/E ratios, glamor stocks sometimes 50 to 1 or more. Toward the close of 1968 the Dow Jones industrial average had a P/E ratio of about 16 to 1.

PROSPECTUS

A printed statement, filed with the SEC, describing the plans and prospects of a business, financial details of the company and of its officers and directors. Mailed to prospective customers and others, the prospectus also describes the terms of becoming a shareholder.

Picking Up the Jargon

PROXY

A request by the management for a stockholder's signed vote on certain items of business to come up at the annual meeting.

QUOTATIONS

A record of the highest bid to buy a stock and the lowest offer to sell at any given time. Daily quotation tables printed in newspapers give the previous day's highest, lowest and closing prices on stocks traded on the New York Stock Exchange and the American Stock Exchange. The price of stocks is listed in 8ths instead of 10ths. A stock can be quoted in three ways:

    10¼   10.25 $10.25

RIGHTS

When a company needs additional capital, it may issue new shares of stock. Before making a public offering, the company may offer its present shareholders the first chance to buy the new shares. The company issues rights to a shareholder based on the number of shares owned. Usually the new stock is offered for less than the current market price. Failure to use or sell the rights within the specified time limit will mean a loss to the shareholder, either in actual cash or his percentage of ownership in the company. The question is whether you want to buy another share at a reduced rate and retain your percentage of ownership, or whether you sell the rights and reduce your cost base.

ROUND LOTS

A unit of trading on the New York and other stock exchanges, usually 100 shares.

SEAT

A membership or the right of a broker to trade shares on one of the stock exchanges. Originally this was a seat, but today no broker sits down to trade. Due to deaths or retirement of members, seats are available from time to time to the highest bidder.

SECURITIES AND EXCHANGE COMMISSION (SEC)

A five-man commission set up by congress to administer the Securities Act of 1933 and the Securities and Exchange Act of 1934. The SEC oversees the registration of securities listed on exchanges, and prohibits fraudulent practices that might deceive the investor.

SHORT SELLING

A person borrows shares from a brokerage firm in order to sell shares he does not own. He must pay for any dividend declared during the time he borrows, and must also put up cash or stock equal to the sale price of the borrowed shares. He does this because he expects, or takes a chance, that the stock will drop. When it drops he buys, returns the stock to his broker, and pockets the profits.

SPECIALIST

Specializes in only a few stocks, or even only one of the larger corporations. More than 25 percent of NYSE members work in this capacity. The specialist stays at the trading post where his special stocks trade, instead of moving about from post to post as other brokers do.

He is often charged with filling limit orders (the buyer or seller sets a limit on the price he will pay or sell for, either lower or higher than the present market price). Regular brokers cannot possibly wait for the market to fall or rise in order to fulfill limit orders.

The specialist makes an "orderly market" in the stocks in which he specializes. Whenever more sell orders appear for one of his stocks than the market has buy orders for, the specialist buys, within reason, some of the stock for his own account. When buyers frantically call for more of one of the stocks he specializes in than the market has to sell, the specialist sells from his own account, thus keeping the market on an even keel. A specialist may have hundreds of thousands of dollars tied up in his own account, and often risks large amounts of his own capital.

In times of sudden disaster or uncertainty such as the assassination of President Kennedy, the capture of *The Pueblo,* Russia's invasion of Czechoslovakia, the specialist attempts to stabilize the market in his particular stocks. In buying or selling from his own account, he minimizes erratic price movements. He makes an orderly market. Heavy in-and-out trading by the institutions often makes the specialist's job highly precarious.

SPECULATION

Taking an informed risk in the hope of gaining larger than ordinary profits. The men who run brokerage firms and stock exchanges make a distinction between investing, speculating, and gambling. The *investor,* they contend, plans an investment program for the future. The investor informs himself and buys high-grade stocks, intending to keep them for the long haul. The investor's goals include regular dividends, safety of capital, and growth of capital. (Experts dispute whether all three can be realized at the same time.)

The *speculator* knowingly takes a greater risk in the stocks he buys. He buys not for dividends or long-term growth but in the hope of quick profits. His chief goal is to make money as quickly as possible, although on occasion he does buy new company stocks with growth potential. In such cases he forgets about the stocks for months, but based on his investigation, he shrewdly expects the stocks to increase in value many times his original cost.

Because the speculator takes more than ordinary risks in the stock he buys, he often makes more than ordinary gains. Similarly he sometimes suffers more than ordinary losses. Most important, as a speculator, he understands the risks he takes and buys only what he can afford to lose.

The *gambler* buys and sells on whims, hot tips, and wild rumors. The gambler favors "chancy," low-priced dollar stocks, hoping for gain. The gambler wants easy money without working for it—a childish hope for magic.

Brokerage firms frown on gambling. Giant brokerage house Merrill Lynch, Pierce, Fenner and Smith, Inc., advertises it refuses "to open accounts for the sole purpose of buying 'penny' (or dollar) stocks."

Any woman gambles who buys stocks without investigating the company or at least relying on the knowledge of her broker or other trustworthy person.

STOCK DIVIDEND

Represents a distribution paid to shareholders in stock rather than cash. This enables the company to retain extra cash for reinvestment in the business.

Suppose a woman holds 100 shares of a certain company. She paid $45 a share for the stock, or $4,500. The company wants more money for research and expansion. It declares a 5 percent stock dividend of one extra share for each 20 shares held. This doesn't mean that the company has handed the woman the equivalent of $225. Nothing is basically changed. True she now holds 105 shares, but her total investment is still $4,500. Her 105 shares still represent the same percentage of ownership in the company as her 100 shares did. She must adjust her cost basis. Instead of 100 shares costing her $4,500, or $45 a share, she now has 105 shares costing her $4,500, or $42.85 a share. She stands to gain if the 105 shares increase in value.

STOCK SPLIT

When a stock splits two-for-one, for example, some stockholders believe they have doubled their equity. But the value of a stock split is mostly psychological. Generally the new price, being less, is more attractive to investors. Some experts tell us that a stock split has no effect on the future price of the shares. When a stock splits two-for-one, a stockholder owns exactly the same amount of investment represented by twice as many shares at half the price of the old stock when it split. An investor does stand to gain in two ways.

1. If after the split the dividend is raised, instead of divided to make it the same amount as paid on the higher priced stock, the stockholder gains.
2. If the demand for the stock is great enough to run up the price between the announcement (or rumor) of the stock split and the actual split, and if the stock stays up after the split, the stockholder gains.

Just before International Business Machine Corporation announced one of its stock splits, the stock, priced at about $622, at once began to climb. Because of anticipated profits buyers scrambled for it. This pushed the price up over $700. When the stock split two-for-one the new price was $361, a fine gain over the price before the announced split. (Later the stock did drop as low as $301 a share.)

STREET NAME

Stocks held in the name of the brokerage firm, who keeps a paper record of them instead of turning the actual certificates over to the investor. The brokerage office credits any dividends to the customer and sends him a monthly statement of his account, as a service.

TENDER OFFER

A corporation's offer to buy up another company or a specific number of shares at a fixed price.

TICKER

A telegraphic receiving instrument that works through a computer, automatically printing stock quotations or news on a paper ribbon called a ticker tape.

TICKER TAPE

After each sale in the stock exchange, a notation of the

sale, name of stock (in code), number of shares traded, and the price is typed on the ticker tape. It is then flashed by wire to brokers' offices from coast to coast. There the ticker tape is blown up and projected on a wall-to-wall screen for all to see. The following, decoded, means that

EK	NAC	UAL
79	52 1/2	35 3/8

100 shares of Eastman Kodak just sold for $79 a share, 100 shares of National Can sold for $52.50 a share, 100 shares of United Air Lines for $35.38 a share.

During high volume days the ticker tape often runs minutes behind.

TRADER

One who buys and sells stocks for a short-term profit. This is a special technique of in-and-out trading that probably requires full-time attention to the brokerage house quotation board in order to watch daily and even hourly stock fluctuations. The trader makes his profits by strategic timing in buying and selling.

TRANSFER AGENT

Usually a large bank or holding company that keeps a record of a corporation's stockholders, certificates, and accepts old certificates for cancellation.

TRANSFER TAX

Levied by New York State and a few others, and paid by the seller whenever stock is sold or transferred to another person. The tax is from one to four cents a share, depending on price.

TREASURY STOCK

Stock once issued for public investment, but later bought back by the company and held in its treasury. Such rebuying of stock is actually partial liquidation of the company, since no dividends are paid on treasury stock. The company may

Picking Up the Jargon

use its treasury stock to reduce cash dividend payments to stockholders, or for employee stock options and purchase plans.

WARRANTS

A warrant holder has the right to buy a certain number of shares at a specified price. The warrant certificate carries an expiration date, or it may give the holder what is known as perpetual rights, the right to buy the shares any time in the future. Warrants are only valuable and a good investment if the company who issues them flourishes.

YIELD

Return on an investment. In other words, dividends as a percentage of market value. To figure current yield for a common stock, divide the total dividends paid the last full year by the current market value of the stock. To figure original investment yield, divide the total dividends paid the last full year by the original cost of the stock.

Many other terms may bob up to puzzle you, such as chartists, convertibles, the Dow theory, pre-emptive rights, puts and calls, short interest. You will find these and many more explained in the New York Stock Exchange's free booklet, "The Language of Investing," which lists nearly 250 words and expressions.

To Benefit Most from This Chapter:

1. In your filing carton set up a folder for averages. Compare the Dow Jones industrial average with Standard and Poor's 500-stock composite. Record these averages each time you record the quotations on your hypothetical stocks.
2. Scan OTC quotations. Do you recognize any companies listed? Do you consider them high-grade or blue chip companies?
3. Check the price range of several OTC stocks. How can you say that many of these are speculative?

How the Stock Market Functions 5

"Dad, I have $200 in the bank," 17-year-old Jimmy told his father. "I want to buy some stock."

"Good for you," his father said. He sat Jimmy down at the kitchen table and began to explain how the stock market works.

"Never mind all that jazz," Jimmy interrupted. "Let's get to the part where I make money."

Like Jimmy, I didn't want to learn all that much about the stock market. I just wanted to make money. I drove a car, didn't I? What I knew about the inside of a car was nebulous. Yet thanks to our modern automobile industry (one in which women invest money) I could drive without a great deal of engine and carburetor know-how.

But it doesn't always work that way, I soon learned, with stocks. Somebody has to oversee a woman's portfolio. Several choices face us.

1. Financial advisor

Many women of substantial worth hire a financial advisor. Most of these are not interested in portfolios of less than $100,000. When I first invested on my own I had about $1,000 to invest so I ruled out paying for advice.

2. Investment funds or mutual funds

In good investment or mutual funds your money is spread

How the Stock Market Functions

over scores of stocks and well managed all for a fee. But I wanted the spice of choosing, buying, and selling my own stocks.

3. Trustworthy broker

Of course you must have the help of a broker (an account executive, his formal title) in order to invest in the stock market. Aside from that, if you have confidence in your broker, you will certainly not go too far wrong depending on him to make selections for you. But you will miss a lot of excitement and satisfaction. I had just begun to walk, you might say, in the stock market, and I didn't want any fatherly figure propping me up!

4. Uninformed leaps

Not a few women leap into the stock market without looking. They buy on hunches, tips, and rumors. Or they wake up feeling good, decide now's the time to buy stocks, any stock. Or a bill comes with a forgotten charge. Needing money they hop out of the market just as blindly.

Certainly no woman need be like the young divorcee we'll call Helen Jensen who inherited $3,000 from her aunt. Ready for instant wealth, Helen jumped right in and bought shares in an electronics corporation. When the market dropped and her stock fell 20 points in a month, Helen panicked and sold.

"The stock market's too risky," she said, $700 poorer than when she bought. Soon after she sold, the price of the electronics stock rose. Now Helen wishes she had informed herself and waited out the market drop.

5. Yourself in charge

From a practical point of view, understanding the importance of the stock market in our economy, how it works, and what influences the market can help you make sensible investments. After all, who knows more about your needs than you? Any woman who puts her mind to it can understand enough about the stock market to make her clear-headed in her own stock choices and decisions.

Of course, in the process you must see, hear, and understand a lot of uninteresting facts, figures, and terms. That computer above the eyebrows, though, can go to work for you. As you read this chapter, think of yourself as a private-eye snooping. Pick up your pen and jot down any items that puzzle you. Answers may pop up in other chapters. Look up mystifying terms in Chapter 4, Picking Up the Jargon. The more I learned about the stock market, the more I wanted to know. The more I learned, the more confidence I gained, and so will you.

What is the stock market? How does it function? What makes it tick?

WHAT THE STOCK MARKET IS

You will soon understand that the hub of it all is the stock exchange—a convenient market place where stocks and bonds in certain industries, businesses, and commodities can be bought and sold, at a commission.

The stock market centers around New York City's Wall Street, international symbol of American finance. About 95 percent of trading in listed securities surges through this center. On Wall Street, only three blocks long, stands the New York Stock Exchange building, the country's largest exchange. The second largest, the American Stock Exchange, is around the corner on Trinity Place. Altogether in the United States there are 13 national exchanges registered with the Securities and Exchange Commission:

American Stock Exchange
Boston Stock Exchange
Chicago Board of Trade
Cincinnati Stock Exchange
Detroit Stock Exchange
Midwest Stock Exchange
National Stock Exchange
New York Stock Exchange
Pacific Stock Exchange
Philadelphia-Baltimore-Washington Stock Exchange (Recently moved outside Philadelphia)
Pittsburgh Stock Exchange
Salt Lake Stock Exchange
Spokane Stock Exchange

How the Stock Market Functions

But the stock market is not only the visible stock exchange building. It is also countless trends, discoveries, disasters, choices, wishful tips, and wild rumors. It is industries, goods, services, money, ticker tapes, and quotations. It is, above all, people who invest, expecting a return on their money.

People who mill around the floor, plus coast-to-coast buyers, employees in brokerage offices, plus seat-members who pay hundreds of thousands of dollars for a seat. People who gamble, speculate, invest. People who compete for a cut in the pie of American business. People who lend their money (hoping to gain, of course) in order that industries and corporations may grow and discover new products or new ways of doing things. People who want more and more things and hope that the economy will keep on rising.

GROSS NATIONAL PRODUCT

One hand that keeps the economy bouncing higher and higher is the tremendous increase in new industries. No one will disagree with the experts who tell us that America has produced more new products, companies, and industries in the past ten years than in any other decade of our country's history.

The market value of all the goods and services produced in the U.S. is calculated by statisticians as the gross national product (GNP). GNP is one of the best indicators of the direction of our economy. GNP soared to spectacular heights in the past decade. It rose from $104 billion in 1929, the first year records were kept, to $504 billion in 1960—up $400 billion in 31 years. From there it rocketed in 1968 to $860 billion, an increase of more than $300 billion in eight years. This, in spite of the fact that not long ago statisticians had set the projected rate of $800 billion for the year 1970.

Still another impetus to America's economic growth is increased population. Our schools creak and bulge with those under 25. More people live longer. Nineteen million today are over 65, the majority with regular social security payments. Those in between enjoy the highest rate of employment and annual income our country has known.

More jobs and higher pay generate a demand for more and better goods and services, a higher standard of living. Even a higher poverty base prevails, with major appliances, TV, and cars deemed essential.

In short, the experts point to three influences that force our economy upward:

1. Increased population, creating more wants and needs.
2. New industries and older ones expanding, resulting in the need for more workers and capital.
3. More jobs and higher pay resulting in higher standards of wants and needs.

It makes sense, then, to agree with economists who tell us America's growth, barring a world wide catastrophe, is not likely to decrease. Plainly, the economy is gaining momentum.

SHAREHOLDERS' PART

What may not be so plain is that right here women come into the picture. In the past men invested private fortunes in American industries and business. Soon more and more companies offered shares of stock to the public in order to finance costly research and new equipment needed for growth. The backing of private fortune proved inadequate to keep pace with the country's surging needs.

Today every shareholder has a part in sustaining our economy. Not only the man or the institution who buys 1,000 shares of stock in a company, or 5,000 or 50,000, helps finance American enterprises. Hundreds and thousands of odd-lot (less than 100 shares) investors and mutual fund owners now provide capital—the push that sends the economy upward.

As stockholders, women can own an interest in the assets and earnings of American industry. If a company grows and profits, so will we, since when a company profits the value of its stock and the amount of its dividend usually go up.

HOW IT ALL BEGAN

Buying shares today, though, is far removed from the way Queen Isabella of Spain invested in Christopher Columbus's historical voyage into the unknown. Nor does modern investing resemble the way Britain's Queen Elizabeth I raised capital for importing spices and tea from the East Indies.

America's stock market sprang up almost 200 years ago when congress authorized an $80 million issue of stock to help pay for the Revolutionary War. This soon led to the need for a special market place to trade securities. In 1792, 24 men stood beneath a sycamore tree on Wall Street and signed an agreement for trading shares. The organization later became the New York Stock Exchange and the basis for today's complex stock market. At first men traded shares person-to-person in a coffee house or a bank and in the street. Banks and insurance companies also put up shares of stock for sale. In the mid-nineteenth century another outdoor market sprang up, the Curb, so named because brokers stood on the curb to trade shares. Later the Curb market became the American Stock Exchange.

HOW THE STOCK MARKET FUNCTIONS

The ideal way to learn about the stock market would be to visit New York City and spend an hour at the American Stock Exchange, or to stand on the glassed-in balcony overlooking the New York Stock Exchange floor. Hundreds of thousands of visitors each year watch the incredible hub-bub of the stock exchange. (If you can't visit a New York exchange, perhaps you are near a regional one. Or visit a nearby brokerage office to get the flavor of the vast system that is the stock market.)

The "floor" of the NYSE is nearly as large as a football field and as disorderly, you might think, as if the spectators had spilled out onto it, until someone explains what is going on. The floor is high-ceilinged, rimmed with direct line phone booths hooked up to brokerage houses across the nation. Activity centers around 19 large, horse-shoe shaped booths, or trading posts. About 75 stocks are traded from each post. Hundreds of men, including messengers, pages, and clerks, as well as members, or seat-owners, scurry back and forth across the floor.

Indispensible in all the activity is the seat-owner, or broker, who must buy a "seat" for the privilege of conducting business on the exchange floor. This usually costs several hundred thousand dollars, besides an initiation fee and annual dues. In 1968 a seat on the NYSE sold for $515,000, and a seat on the AMEX sold for a record high of $300,000. The highest price ever paid for a seat was $725,000 for one on the New York Stock Exchange back in 1929.

Originally this was a seat. Brokers sat as they listened to the day's list or quotation of stocks offered. Now there is too much activity on the floor for a broker to sit. Instead he shuttles swiftly across the floor between phone, trading post, and other brokers. He shouts, writes on scraps of paper, and litters the floor with discarded scraps. (At the close of each day workmen sweep off the floor more than a ton of waste paper.)

Along the wall the huge electric quote board, of interest to all who visit the exchange, runs a cumulative report on the listed stocks traded, identified by code letters. Computers record price changes and the number of shares only moments after a trade. Brokers, to avoid manipulation of the market, hold the names of buyer and seller in strict confidence. Ticker department accountants compile and report to the press the day's business, known as the market list or stock quotations.

How the Stock Market Functions

Some refer to the stock exchange as a two-way auction. The noise and confusion of the exchange floor does sound like an auction. More than 1,000 "auctioneers," or brokers, tramp the floor of the NYSE. Buyers compete for the lowest price and sellers for the highest price.

NEW YORK STOCK EXCHANGE

The NYSE, often called "The Big Board," referring to the number of shares listed, traded, and flashed to the electric board, lists about 1,300 business enterprises. All have passed the Securities and Exchange Commission's requirements for listing on a national exchange. At least three times in 1968 the volume of shares traded on the NYSE reached 20 million, surpassing the previous all-time high of 16 million shares traded in 1929 when the market crashed.

AMERICAN STOCK EXCHANGE

Sales on the AMEX, formerly referred to as "The Little Board," also rocketed to all-time highs in 1968. As many as 10 million shares a day traded hands.

Brokers also trade listed shares in the various regional exchanges and trade in grain and animal markets.

OVER-THE-COUNTER MARKET

All the rest of the stocks, estimated at around 30,000, are traded in the over-the-counter market (OTC). The term carries over from early days when men actually traded the stock over a bank's counter. Most of the stocks sold OTC fail to meet national exchange requirements of size and profits, with a few notable exceptions, such as most bank and insurance stocks, U.S. government bonds, and other high-grade bonds.

Through the OTC market a company first offers its shares of stock to the public. As soon as the company meets the Securities and Exchange Commission's requirements, it can apply to be listed on a national exchange. (Requirements of the NYSE are stricter than those of AMEX. Thus many more speculative stocks are listed on the American Stock Exchange.) Unlike the national exchanges, trading in OTC stocks marches on without a central market place, though dealers tend to center in New York City. Brokerage firms conduct business with OTC dealers by private phones and Teletype lines. (See previous discussion of OTC stocks in Chapter 4, Picking Up the Jargon.)

MECHANICS OF BUYING AND SELLING

How does a woman go about investing her money in someone else's business? Suppose a woman in Two Harbors, Minnesota, wants to buy 20 shares of Avon Products. How does she break into the tumultuous auctioning of the stock exchange? As one of 26 million shareholders in America, she would find it impossible to deal directly with the exchange or to visit it each time she wanted to buy stocks. Instead she deals with a brokerage firm, either through her local bank or by going to a nearby city with a branch brokerage office, in her case, Duluth.

Brokerage firms, or member firms, usually have head offices in New York City, and branches in scores of cities. Merrill Lynch, Pierce, Fenner and Smith, the largest brokerage house, runs more than 300 branch offices in the United States, and in such widely spaced foreign countries as Paris, Rome, London, Hong Kong, and Beruit.

First our Two Harbors woman goes to the nearest brokerage office, explains she wants to buy some stock, and asks for an account executive. Even if she is only trying to learn, it won't cost anything. Brokerage houses are eager to open new accounts. Of course our hypothetical woman will have to give business references, as in any other charge account. You buy stocks with a five-day grace period to pay for new shares or to deliver shares you want to sell. Before the heavy volume of recent years and the resulting jam of paper work, transfer

How the Stock Market Functions

agents usually delivered, or at least issued, new stock certificates within the grace period. Now it takes much longer, sometimes weeks or months. If our woman also explains her goals and needs in investing, the account executive, or broker, can be of greater help.

On the broker's desk stands a stock quote machine connected to a computer system in the NYSE. The broker can ask for and instantly receive facts and figures on any listed stock, such as the year's highest and lowest prices, price at the moment, company earnings, dividends, and price-earnings ratio. If the woman considers the quoted price satisfactory she places a buy order, which is sent by Teletype to the New York brokerage office.

The firm's broker on the floor of the exchange is the go-between for regular lot orders of 100 shares or more. Since our hypothetical woman in Two Harbors wants fewer than 100 shares, an odd-lot dealer handles the transaction. He groups together other odd-lot orders and then deals with the broker on the floor in 100 share lots. As soon as the broker on the floor receives the buy order from his New York office, or an odd-lot dealer, he hurries to the trading post where Avon Products is traded and bargains. A broker who has a sell order, perhaps from his Dallas, Texas, office, offers the stock for sale. Brokers must call their bids and offers out loud, not secretly.

Trading in the stock market entails not only selling, as one woman mistakenly thought, but buying as well.

"What shall I do?" she frantically asked her broker. "General Motors stock is going down. Everybody's selling!" She failed to understand that probably other people were buying just as many shares as those who were selling. If the stock dropped a point or more because hundreds of owners wanted to sell, the very fact of the drop in price might make it attractive to hundreds of others.

On the exchange floor, buyer and seller often not more than half a point apart, agree on the price. Next each broker relays the details of the trade to his brokerage firm. Another trade flashes onto the electric board, relayed to branch offices. All this takes only a short time, often a matter of seconds from the time the woman placed her order until she can know the stock is hers. The brokerage office mails the woman a confirmation slip. (Hold onto it! You need it for tax records and resale.) The seller delivers his stock certificate and receives his check. In due time the transfer agent mails out the actual stock certificate. Or our Two Harbors woman may choose to leave her stock certificate with the brokerage house—in the street's name—who will send her a monthly statement and mail dividends to her as a service. (More of this in Chapter 12, Keeping Essential Records.)

With little effort on her part at this point, our imaginary woman is a new stockholder.

WHAT ABOUT SAFETY?

You may be asking, "How do I know there won't be another market crash like the one in 1929?" I found myself smack up against a road block when I thought about this question until I delved a bit. Any woman's money, I knew, represents hard work, on her husband's part, on her own, or someone else's. And from my husband's teaching I had come to respect money. The ability to earn it, or even the gift of money, carries with it the responsibility to protect it and use it properly.

Can a woman be reasonably sure of the safety of her money in the stock market? Brokerage houses and the stock exchanges are the first to admit that investing in the stock market carries a certain amount of risk.

Already I had experienced the sad fact of life that a lot of people are out to make money from gullible single women, divorcees, and widows. Yet as I talked to other women I found many of them with sound business sense, not to be taken in by wild tips and rumors or high-pressure salesmanship. Women don't "gull" as easily as in the past. Women are inquisitive, not content to glide over issues. When it comes to their own money they want straightforward answers.

PROTECTION OF SECURITIES AND EXCHANGE COMMISSION

One positive answer is that the government, stock exchanges, and business itself are working to prevent a recurrence of the 1929 crash. They don't want it any more than we do. The Securities Acts of 1933 and 1934 set the system on a firm base. The Securities and Exchange Commission (SEC), a five-man federal committee, keeps tabs on the stock exchanges, brokerage houses, and the market in order to protect the investor. To rig, bribe, or manipulate stock prices is rated a criminal offense. When the SEC suspects duplicity it steps in with public investigation.

The SEC requires corporations listed on national exchanges to declare the truth about their finances, to mail honest financial reports to stockholders. When requesting a proxy (absentee ballot), the company must reveal the number of shares held by and salaries paid its officers and directors.

To guard investors SEC has, on occasion, blocked all trading on certain speculative stocks and raised the margin on listed stock to, at present, 80 percent. But this is not all. Even the exchanges must be registered with the SEC. A president and a board of governors head the exchange today in contrast to the loose system before the 1929 crash.

Also important, the exchanges themselves police trading, checking members by computer or suspending trading on a stock if it no longer meets SEC requirements. Take the way AMEX banned not long ago margin trading on one stock, and finally all trading on it in order to reduce unexplained speculation in that stock.

Heavy speculation, in-and-out trading, and huge volume resulted in bookkeeping and paper work in exchange offices in 1968 that threatened to bury the system. Brokerage offices fell days behind in stock records and certificate deliveries. Because "fails" (failure to deliver a certificate within the grace period) were common, transfer agents took weeks and months to issue new certificates. To dig out, the NYSE and the AMEX closed an hour and a half early each business day, and for months closed all day Wednesdays. Mid-year the NYSE instituted computerized delivery of certificates, wherein ownership of shares changed between brokers without physical movement or change of the certificates.

With such regulations, the authorities believe a repeat of the 1929 disaster unlikely. At that time low ethical standards and excessive credit prevailed. Salesmen and buyers, greedy to get rich quick, often gambled their own credit right out the window.

Despite certain open and hidden risks in the stock market, buying common stocks is one way a woman can protect and increase her capital. To do this takes faith that America will continue to prosper, that American business will continue to grow.

WHY THE MARKET FLUCTUATES

Another question that may trouble you is: What makes stock prices jump up and down? The law of supply and demand keeps the market fluctuating. When more shareholders want to sell stocks than others want to buy, the market goes down. When more buyers want stocks than others want to sell, the price spurts up. War, a ship held in enemy waters, failure of congress to pass a tax increase, urban unrest, a drop in a company's earnings—any of these can cause individual stocks to sag, as well as the market as a whole. A cut in interest rates, hope that the war will end, a report of higher incomes on a national level, high price-earnings, mergers--these can cause the market to soar. And a certain intangible—uncertainty, public opinion, or what people think or feel about the market as a whole or about individual corporations—can also shoot the market up or drag it down.

How the Stock Market Functions

Knowing this can help you as a shareowner to remain calm on bad-news days and not to go out and buy a chinchilla coat the first day the market climbs. To intelligently buy common stocks on your own from time to time requires understanding how the complex stock market functions. It takes understanding how various economical, political, technical, and even emotional factors influence the rise and fall of the market.

Such knowledge will give you a toe in the door to choosing your own stocks. It will also give you a gold-sprayed ball to toss into any group when conversation bogs down. The next time you are with friends, toss the subject of the stock market into the group. Watch the eyebrows soar like the price of shares on a rumored stock split.

More important, as your knowledge grows and you select stocks in sound progressive companies and retain them as long as they perform well, you will protect and increase your capital in spite of higher taxes and shrinking dollars. Increased capital will make it easier to shoulder future responsibilities such as education, retirement, your obligations to the church and the world's needy.

Any woman who has faith that America will continue to prosper, that American business will keep on growing, will want to put some of her capital into common stocks.

To Benefit Most from This Chapter:

1. Visit a stock exchange if possible. If not, visit a brokerage office.
2. Sit in one of the chairs provided for visitors and watch the electric quote board. Do you recognize any of the symbols that flash across the board?
3. Has anything happened in the news nationally or worldwide that might cause the market to drop or rise, either now or in the future?
4. Introduce the subject of securities and the stock market into at least two group situations.

How to Read a Financial Report

6

Soon after the close of the year, American business enterprises flood the mails with their annual financial reports. Some corporations conduct business on a fiscal year other than the calendar year, usually ending June 30, and so send their annual reports later.

The Securities and Exchange Commission requires all listed companies to send these yearly financial reports to stockholders. What is not required is the colorful slick paper publication that most corporations mail out. Companies vie with one another to print the most alluring report. As eye-catching as any periodical that comes into your house, the annual report deserves a careful reading. It needs to be cracked, and the meat picked out like that of any walnut.

Like most women of integrity you probably expect a fair deal in business transactions. You buy curtains at your favorite department store. The curtains shrink and fray, so you complain, and the store refunds your money.

Not so when you buy shares of stock. Instead you buy a cut of a corporation, and you stand to lose or gain with that corporation. Nothing guarantees satisfaction or your money back. "Let the buyer beware," is an old warning, but it holds true today in the securities market. Before you buy stock take a hard look at the way the company operates. Why accept ready-mix answers when you can learn on your own by studying a corporation's annual report?

Of course the figures in millions and billions of dollars, the percentages and ratios are clear to bookkeepers and accountants who work with figures all day, and who compile the reports. Company officials, too, have trained themselves to understand a financial report at a glance. This is their business.

We women, who at first may be beyond our depth with a financial report, can take heart. The saying: More people are skillful because of long practice than as a result of inborn talent holds true when it comes to these reports. Each professional was once an amateur. Most men turned loose in a woman's kitchen might flounder, too. Almost any man asked to order ingredients for, prepare and serve dinner for eight would either try to escape or turn to cook books and etiquette books and a little womanly help.

In the same way, time spent studying your company's financial report will help you understand its format and meaning. You may also discover important clues and tips, messages and foreshadowing about the company's prospects. The figures at first glance may appear mysterious, but they need not remain a mystery to you. And after you master two or three such reports, you will understand others, since most of them more or less follow a pattern.

IMPROVED FORMAT HELPFUL

Many corporations consider it a matter of integrity to issue straightforward reports to shareholders. Still it is only natural for a company to present its financial condition in a favorable light, and to play down anything unfavorable. Despite SEC requirements that each corporation listed on a national exchange file a copy of its annual report with the commission, and that figures for earnings and financial position be truthfully presented, annual reports come in for criticism from time to time. Occasionally, human nature being what it is, officials arrange or emphasize figures in a report so that they appear to say one thing when such is not the case. Comparison of a company's annual reports for several years and of other similar industries can sometimes point up differences.

In policing securities the SEC undertakes to open the eyes of investors to any irregularities in the market. The rest is up to the investor.

In addition, in 1967 the American Institute of Certified Public Accountants insisted on new rules regarding earnings per share in corporation reports. For example, all convertible stock outstanding must be shown fully converted in the annual report. Also, corporations must present their reports in simpler form so that not only the sophisticated investor can understand, but the small beginner as well. (Big day for us!)

WHAT TO LOOK FOR

Perhaps you have at hand two or three annual reports. If not, a broker may be able to supply you, though possibly not the particular reports you want. Flip the pages to "Highlights" (sometimes termed "Financial Highlights," or "Operating Highlights"). This digest of your company's affairs lists figures side by side for the year just ended and the previous year. At a glance you can compare the company's performance.

Next look at the back of the publication for the auditor's report. When an independent certified accounting firm signs a corporation's report, you may assume that the figures, as far as they go, are truthful and accurate.

Then turn to the pages of figures. Although various corporations report annual figures under different headings, two basic reports concern us:

1. Balance Sheet (or Statement of Financial Position)

The balance sheet shows assets and liabilities, or the condition of the company on the last day of its fiscal year.

2. Statement of Income (or Statement of Operations and Statement of Source and Application of Funds)

How to Read a Financial Report

The statement of income shows sales for the year, where the income came from, and what the company did with it. Some companies report these figures all in one statement. Others break it up into two or three.

I used to wonder why financial reports always balance. Assets equal liabilities—not a penny left over. Things never came out that way with my household accounts. But I soon learned that in business bookkeeping everything always comes out balanced. If you stop to figure it out, personal bookkeeping does the same.

What you get paid for working, from pensions, what you withdraw from savings, what you borrow from the bank or Uncle Chester, all must add up to what you pay for rent, groceries, taxes, transportation, savings and everything else you spend money for. If it doesn't you're in trouble.

Let's see why.

INCOME	OUTGO
(All the money you take in)	(Everything you spend money for)
Pay check	Rent
Interest on savings accounts	Groceries
Dividends on investments	Clothing, medical expense, charity
Money borrowed	
Other sources: Pension or insurance, gifts, awards	Transportation
	Taxes
	Savings and investments

The two columns *must* balance. If you pay out more than you take in, you're operating in the red.

In the case of a corporation, income must balance with costs and expenses. Total assets equal total liabilities, plus stockholders' equity (their investment in the company). The corporation reports these figures on two separate statements—the balance sheet and the statement of income. The balance sheet shows the financial condition of the company on one certain day, usually the last business day of the year. The income statement reports all money the company received, the way it spent the money, and how much is left over for the year. Both of these reports show a comparison of figures for the year just ended and the previous year. As you study ask yourself: What do these reports have to say about the company's present condition and its future prospects?

SAMPLE BALANCE SHEET

ASSETS

Current Assets
    Cash and interest bearing bank deposits
    Marketable securities and accrued interest
    Accounts receivable, less reserve for bad debts
    Other receivables
    Inventories
        Finished goods, work in process (at market or cost, whichever is lower)
        Raw materials and supplies
                Total current assets

Investments
    Company common stock held for stock option plans (treasury stock)
    Investments in subsidiaries not consolidated
                Total investments

Fixed Assets
    (Plant and equipment at cost)
    Land
    Buildings and leasehold improvements
    Machinery and equipment
                Total plant and equipment
    Less accumulated depreciation
                Plant and equipment net

Other Assets
    (including patents and trademarks)
    Good will
    Prepaid expenses
                Total Other Assets
                TOTAL ASSETS

LIABILITIES

Current Liabilities
    Notes and accounts payable
    Payrolls
    Accrued income taxes, including deferred taxes
    Other taxes and liabilities
    Current portion of long-term debt (due within one year)
                       Total current liabilities

Long-Term Debt
    Mortgages
    Bonds
    Obligations of subsidiaries (if consolidated)
                       Total long-term debt

Stockholders' Investment
    Preferred stock
    Common stock (no par value)
    Net income retained for use in the business
    Capital surplus or paid in capital
                       Total stockholders'
                             investment
                TOTAL LIABILITIES

Open the annual report to the balance sheet. (Balance sheets and income statements often drop the last three digits of their figures for easier reading.) On the left-hand page you'll find the company's assets. On the right-hand page, the liabilities. Footnotes are important. They are, as frequently stated, a part of the total financial report and should not be ignored.

    CURRENT ASSETS

Cash on hand, money in the bank, U.S. Government bonds or other securities. Anything included in cash can be quickly liquidated, usually within a year from the date of the balance sheet.

Accounts receivable (sometimes called *customer receivables* or *trade receivables* are amounts due from customers in 30, 60, or 90 days for goods already shipped—

charge accounts. After the term *accounts receivable* you'll find an amount subtracted as a provision for bad debts. Business customers, as well as individuals, sometimes run into financial trouble and fail to pay their bills. For this reason the corporation sets up an estimated allowance for unpaid bills, and deducts this from its accounts receivable.

Inventories consist of raw materials and supplies, work in process, finished products on hand, all reported at cost of materials and production. Otherwise when the time came to sell the product, variables such as heavy competition might cause the inventories to slump.

Investments include any lesser companies in foreign countries or in different enterprises the corporation owns. Because the assets and liabilities of such subsidiary companies might not reflect a true picture of the parent company, they often are not included in its financial report, but explained in a footnote. Often, though, such subsidiary companies are included in what is known as a consolidated balance sheet and statement of income.

Again when a corporation invests money in a joint venture with another corporation, these figures do not appear in detail in the annual report. For example, American Can Company in a footnote to its 1967 report explained one part of its investments by stating the company was "a participant in an unincorporated joint venture" with another major company.

FIXED ASSETS

Under this heading would come land, buildings, office equipment, production machinery, delivery equipment—all more or less permanent or long-term assets. Depreciation on these items is deducted over a period of years, except in the case of land, which cannot be easily determined.

Other assets, including good will, which has to do with the number of customers, their loyalty to the company's products or service. Also included you'll find any patents, and estimate of the value of the company's name. Since good will is, of course, an intangible and difficult to evaluate, various companies report it in different ways. American Can Company valued its good will at $6,052 (1967), International Business Machines at $1. Other corporations simply do not include the item at all.

Across the page from Assets, you'll find Liabilities. The ratio between current assets and current liabilities tells us about the soundness of the company. We'll see why later.

CURRENT LIABILITIES

Bills and contracts the company must pay before the year is up, such as wages, salaries, pensions, notes to banks, dividends to stockholders, taxes, and any part or interest on a long-term debt due within the year.

LONG-TERM OR FIXED LIABILITIES

The amount a company owes to others for longer than one year. The value of bonds outstanding, installments, mortgages.

Common stock means the amount paid into the company for its common stock.

Capital surplus means the amount paid in for stock above its par value.

Net income retained means the amount of earnings above dividends paid out that the company retained for its own use, research, and expansion.

Doubtless you'll recall the theory of compounding money. Say you have $500 in the bank at 4 percent interest, or in a Savings and Loan company at 5 percent interest, either one compounded quarterly. If you leave the money there and allow the interest to remain on deposit, your money will double at 4 percent in 18 years, at 5 percent in 14 years. In somewhat the same manner, retained earnings help to compound the capital, or value of a corporation.

The figure for earned surplus or retained earnings is cumulative. By comparing the figure for several years (find the four- or five-year summary in the annual report) you will learn whether the figure has gradually increased, rapidly increased, or remained static.

A steady growth in retained earnings probably means that the company has not only paid out dividends to stockholders each year, but by plowing back part of its earnings it becomes financially stronger.

Substantial growth in retained earnings probably points to the fact that shareholders receive little or no dividends, but by reinvesting most of its earnings the company grows rapidly.

Retained earnings that show no change may mean the company pays out most of its earnings in dividends, thus cutting its own ability for growth.

A company may even use its retained earnings in time of depression or a year of loss to pay a dividend.

Because the term "par value" is generally misunderstood and has lost its significance, many companies set a very low value, $1 or $5, on a share of stock. Some corporations do not attach any par or stated value to their stock.

Book value, a term some corporations list in their reports, has also come to have less meaning than previously. In a period of inflation, public opinion can run up the price of the stock far above its book value. On the other hand the stock of companies with huge investments in equipment often sells for less than book value. The earning power of a company means more than either par or book value.

PRESIDENT CHATS WITH SHAREHOLDERS

Next turn to the president's remarks to stockholders, found near the front of the booklet. You'll understand what he has to say better now that you've studied the balance sheet. In the president's letter you may find pointers, hints, predictions about the company's prospects for the next year. Does he state that net sales have increased or established a record? Or have profits dropped because of a non-recurring loss or a labor strike? Is management planning new buildings or branching out into modern problems, such as research in water or air pollution? One company which built two huge structures in one year admitted a strain on cash assets. Instead of increasing dividends, it paid the regular dividend and declared a 5 percent stock dividend, a device for placating stockholders when earnings are good and cash is short.

Also scan the colorful pages that report what the company is doing, its plans for the future, new research, new products or inventions.

BACK TO THE BALANCE SHEET

What can we learn about a company from its balance sheet? For one, you'll find that comparing current assets and current liabilities can point up the soundness of your company.

Net working capital (or net current assets)

Current liabilities must be paid out of current assets. Suppose the company you are investigating paid all its current debts or liabilities from out of its current assets. The balance represents the net working capital. Check to see whether the net working capital is more or less in proportion to liabilities than a year ago.

Too slim a net working capital hampers a corporation from expanding or taking advantage of opportunities. You know how it goes—the once-a-year sale of name-dresses, but you already have charged more than you can conveniently pay for this month, and the check book shows only a few dollars. *Result:* You miss a good bargain.

Just what is a safe amount of working capital for a corporation? In its booklet "How to Read a Financial Report," Merrill Lynch states that most experts agree that for an industrial corporation to be of investment caliber, not speculative, its current assets should be at least twice as large as current liabilities.

To arrive at the ratio between current assets and current liabilities, you divide current assets by current liabilities. For example, Company A in its annual report for 1968 showed:

$$\frac{\text{Current assets}}{\text{Current liabilities}} \quad \frac{\$473{,}454{,}000}{161{,}249{,}000} = \frac{2.9}{1} \text{ or a ratio of 2.9 to 1}$$

Exceptions to the rule of assets twice as large as liabilities would be companies with small inventories and easily collectible accounts. On the other hand, a company with current assets three or four times as great as liabilities may be sitting on the shareholders' money instead of using it for expansion or research.

Leverage stocks

A company is considered high leveraged when it must pay a large amount of bond interest and preferred stock dividends. In a poor year little might remain for common stock dividends or to retain for company expansion.

Those who know state that no more than 25 percent of a company's stock should be in bonds and that the total of bonds and preferred stock should be less than the total of common stock. The reason: Bonds are debts that must be paid. Dividends on preferred stock must be paid before dividends on common stock. Should a company fail, both bonds and preferred stock must be paid for before anything is paid to common stockholders.

Although such stocks appeal to speculators, the conservative investor will steer clear of high leveraged stocks.

From the balance sheet then, we learn something about a company's financial soundness, its ability to meet its obligations at the end of the company's fiscal year.

A LOOK AT THE INCOME STATEMENT

From the income statement you learn how a company spent its money the past year, whether it made a profit or a loss for the year and how much, whether it earned more money than the previous year, and the company's prospects for the future. Of course, even before the annual reports reach you, you'll read in the papers about such pointers on the top ten companies or any others heavily traded; for instance, on IBM, ATT, General Motors, Control Data, Zerox. But the stocks of smaller, high-grade companies may also interest you, and it pays to understand what the income statement can reveal.

Mere size in a company is not everything. A company may have millions of shares outstanding and report hundreds of millions of dollars in sales, and still not be the best investment for the woman who wants to protect and increase her capital. Public opinion may have run up the price of the stock so it is overpriced. In a smaller high-grade company, with only several hundred thousand shares outstanding, even a small profit may mean the company has good potential growth and should be considered as an investment.

SAMPLE INCOME STATEMENT

Sales and other income
    Net sales and other revenue
    Investments, royalties, and other income
                                              Total

Cost of goods sold and other expenses
    Costs and other operating expenses
    Depreciation
    Provision for income taxes
                                              Total

Net income for the year (net profit)
    Net income retained for use at beginning of year
Dividends paid on Common stock
Net income retained for use at end of year
                                              TOTAL

Things to check

    Sales   Profit margin
    Dividends (yield)   Price-earnings ratio

You might compare various other ratios and percentages on the income statement, but for a beginning, let's check the above.

SALES

Compare these on the summary statement which gives figures for four or five years or longer. Have sales climbed steadily? Increase in sales is commendable, of course, but did the company also operate economically with the increased business?

PROFIT MARGIN (PRE-TAX)

Sometimes termed *operating profit,* this is the amount of return the company makes on each dollar of sales. By deducting all operating costs from sales and dividing that figure by sales, you arrive at the operating profit (net profit divided by net sales equals operating profit or profit margin). Compare this figure for several years. Compare it also with the profit margin of other companies doing similar business. Different industries come up with different profit margins. Drug companies, as a rule, show a higher profit margin than food companies.

DIVIDENDS OR YIELD

Most women stockholders like to see their dividends increase, but that in itself is not a sign of a good investment. Possibly the company pays out all its earnings in dividends, leaving nothing for expansion or research. Another company may consistently retain earnings and issue stock dividends instead. Such earned surplus enables it to avoid borrowing money for expansion or new product research at present high interest rates.

To compute the price-dividend ratio, known as the yield, divide the dividend by the current price. Future dividends depend largely on the company's ability to earn money, whether all of it is paid out to stockholders or part retained.

PRICE-EARNINGS RATIO

Figured by dividing the market price of a share by the earnings per share. Earnings per share appear on the financial report. What runs up the price of any stock is belief that the company will continue to increase its earnings per share. The price-earnings ratio holds top place in evaluating the stock of a corporation. In a good growth company you can expect earnings to double every five to seven years. Any decline in earnings should be checked. Besides a good P/E ratio, some authorities now put stress on the assets of a corporation, since some giant blue chip companies have also had consistent growth—IBM, Eastman Kodak.

Twenty years ago experts considered a P/E ratio of 10 to 1 about right, making a stock that sold for ten times its earnings per share a good investment. In mid-1960's the DJ industrial average price-earnings ratio stood at 16 times earnings. At the same time office equipment stocks as a group sold for a much higher price-earnings ratio. Some glamor stocks sold at 50, 60, and even 100 times earnings. Such fantastic ratios depend a great deal on public opinion— what investors expect a corporation to earn in the future. For this reason, many sound stocks, though once good buys, are now overpriced and not considered the best investments for women who want to see their capital increase.

A rising price-earnings ratio pays off in two ways. First, it attracts buyers like a one-hour sidewalk sale. The assumption that everybody's buying sends flocks of investors to the market. Hundreds of buyers competing for shares of the stock push the price up. Shareholders become elated. Second, management (holders of executive stock options who bought company stock at advantageous prices) work to keep price-earnings ratios rising. They see the company stock more and more in demand, the price rising, and when they tote up their stock holdings, the adding machine shows: Gain (at least a paper gain).

Price-earnings ratios, says one security analyst, "have a way of keeping management on its toes." Alert management has cause to worry when the price-earnings ratio drops.

Understanding and figuring these ratios will give you basic skills for investing your own money.

Naturally a corporation compiles its annual report with the intent to show the company in the best possible light. At the same time, the NYSE and AMEX require listed firms to make accurate financial reports. The SEC requires accurate statements. Public accounting firms further check on the accuracy of the annual report. Still it's up to us to interpret the figures and to find out what they mean to us as women shareholders.

If you still have questions about your company's performance, ring up your broker. Most of the ratios and percentages above are at his fingertips.

YOU'RE INVITED TO THE ANNUAL MEETING

To derive benefit from annual meetings, you needn't emulate several notorious stockholders who show up at annual meetings across the country as a full-time avocation. These professional objectors to management own varying amounts of stocks, often only a few shares, in 50 to 200 companies. By heckling and questioning presiding officers at such meetings they stir things up a bit, so reducing the chances of a cut and dried meeting. The avowed purpose, though, of such objectors is to make stockholders aware that "companies are getting away with too much." Sometimes these objectors create enough disturbance to warrant being ousted.

More and more companies, aware of the importance of good public relations, try to make annual meetings informative and interesting. Large corporations use closed circuit TV in the meeting room, hand out free samples of new products, and provide coffee or even box lunches for stockholders.

At an annual meeting you'll have a chance to vote on routine business (usually done ahead of time by proxy vote), according to the number of your shares. The vote of the man with 10,000 shares carries more weight, naturally, than your vote of only 20 shares.

Stockholders do have certain rights at meetings which management recognizes even without professional gadflies. A corporation's officers usually try to give either in advance or at the annual meeting such basic information as whether sales and earnings have increased, plans for research and expansion, major operating or labor problems, salaries of all officers.

Try to attend an annual meeting of some corporation home-based in your locality or near enough to drive. If you live near the home office or the annual meeting place (not always the same) of any of the companies you are watching, by all means try to get permission to attend. (Perhaps your broker can help you.) Your newspaper's financial page usually reports business transacted after the meeting. If you actually own shares you will receive notice of the annual meeting and be asked to sign a proxy vote.

With all this in mind, any woman who wants to protect and increase her capital invested in common stocks should study the annual report of her companies. By now you doubtless sense, if you did not before, the competition that exists in the business world—the obstacles, the failures or successes in individual companies. Only as a company heads into the demands of the future—only as the company grows and prospers—will its stock also increase in value.

To Benefit Most from This Chapter:

1. Obtain at least three annual reports with which to work.
2. Compare the net assets and net liabilities of one company. What is the net working capital?
3. Do the same with the two other financial reports. Compare all three with each other.

4. Compare what the presidents of each company have to say to the stockholders.
5. How many shares outstanding does each company have?
6. What is the present price per share of each company?
7. What is the price-earnings ratio of each company share?

What You Can Learn from Investment Clubs   7

Because many investors like togetherness, investment clubs have zoomed into national popularity. A group of 12 to 15 friends, neighbors, acquaintances from work, church or other organizations form a legal partnership, meeting once a month, for the purpose of investing in the stock market.

Master-minding thousands of successful clubs is the nonprofit organization, the National Association of Investment Clubs. NAIC methods and formula encourage members to work hard at increasing their capital. As a result member clubs expect to, and on the average do, chalk up at least 14 percent annual increase in the money they invest as a club. Put another way, they double their money in five years—an enviable achievement.

Certainly the criticism that "Investment clubs are a bunch of women club members who know absolutely nothing about investing, but yearn for magic," is not justified. Club members may start out knowing little or nothing about investing, but through group interaction and the homework it takes to follow NAIC rules, they become investors with know-how.

Even if you prefer going it alone, what you learn about NAIC methods and its minimum standards for successful investing will benefit you.

WHAT THE NAIC OFFERS YOU

But you may decide the investment club way is for you,

especially if you like the built-in persuader of regular investing, usually $10 or $20 a month per member. You may also like the fine record of growth in capital that most NAIC clubs tick off for themselves. Recent reports show a 16 percent growth of capital, compounded annually, over the last ten years.

At the outset, though, you should understand that joining an investment club is not a hot line to success in the market. An investment club is a partnership, and any woman who joins a club must get behind it and push with the rest of her partners. This requires diligent study, painstaking investigation. You may land smack in the middle of a reporting or debating situation for which you have little training or inclination. But you can learn. It's a hobby at which you *must* work. It's *your* money at stake. If some clubs can increase their capital 15 percent and more a year, why not yours?

Though investment clubs have been around a number of decades, what lifted them off the launching pad was the formation in 1951 of the National Association of Investment Clubs.[1] Today NAIC lists some 11,000 clubs out of an estimated 55,000 in existence. Most of the latter sprang up with advice and help from brokers, but since they function without any overall organization, it's difficult to talk about their success.

Membership in NAIC requires annual dues of $10 for the club itself and $1.50 for each member. In turn each member gets a subscription to the association's monthly magazine, *Better Investing*, and a $25,000 fidelity bond for the club. The association prints a how-to manual, offers all manner of advice, and helps to keep statistics. For instance, polls show that 96 percent of member clubs who answer NAIC questionnaires report an increase on capital invested.

Some clubs operating for a dozen years or more own partnership portfolios of three or four hundred thousand dollars. One long-standing club claims holdings worth over a million dollars.

[1] 13th Floor Washington Blvd. Bldg., Detroit, Michigan 48231.

NAIC GUIDELINES

One part of the NAIC success formula stipulates that all dividends and capital gains from sale of any stock be reinvested rather than paid to club members. Experience shows that by this means an investor who puts in $10 or $20 a month, compounding all dividends and capital gains, can pile up $20,000 in stocks in about 20 years. In one club, a member who has invested just $6,000 over the past 29 years, and for various reasons drew out $10,000, still has $84,000 left. Small wonder investment clubs flourish.

When a club starts, NAIC advises each member to put in the same monthly amount. Later those who have the cash can invest in multiples of the set amount. Or, as is more often the case, members open personal accounts with the brokerage firm and invest on the side, benefiting from the club's pooled knowledge and research.

HOW TO START A CLUB

Do such achievements excite you? Are you asking: How can I get into an investment club? Sometimes because of a member's moving out of town, a death, or other reason, a club does have an opening. You might ask your broker if he knows of one in any of the clubs he counsels. The easiest way, though, to join an investment club is to start one of your own.

Talk the subject at work, at church, with your friends and relatives. Send for the NAIC manual, price $3, and read it. If your new club expects to equal the gains of other clubs of NAIC, it will have to follow the rules.

Try to get together women with a variety of skills and interests. Perhaps one will be a bookkeeper, a fine skill to have in your investment club. Another might be an office clerk, efficient at details. A capable housewife's special skill might be her knowledge of brand names and new products. A teacher, good at research or explaining ideas, would enrich the group. Pick for members women who will be congenial, dependable, and willing to learn and work for the club's success. The club must work together as a team.

CALL THE FIRST MEETING

1. When you know of eight or nine women who want to form an investment club, set a date for the first meeting.

2. At least two or three of you should read the NAIC manual beforehand, especially sections I and II, and be ready to anwer questions about investment clubs.

3. Perhaps by the time of the meeting those who want to form a club may have suggested other women, and you may have a dozen or more prospects. Close the door at 15. Oldtimers believe 12 to 15 members the ideal number for a club. Everyone can work at some phase of stock-buying—as an officer, on a committee, as an accountant or appraiser. Most homes can accommodate 15 people for the monthly meeting. Fewer than 12 members puts a heavy burden on some members. On the other hand, some states prohibit large investment clubs, labeling them investment companies instead. Also, with more than 15 members monthly stock reports might take too much time.

4. Make copies of the partnership agreement in advance of the meeting, so each member can take a copy home for study. A sample partnership agreement is in the manual. (See the manual for full details on a club's first meeting, including setting a regular time for the monthly meeting, 12 months a year, the amount of monthly investment by each member, selection of the club's broker.)

SECOND MEETING

1. Invite either a broker or an experienced investment club member to come to answer questions. The sooner you sign your broker-club agreement the better. (Sample form in the manual.) In choosing a broker, visit the local firm and ask to speak to a man who specializes in investment clubs. He is the man you will work with as a club. If it is not convenient for him to meet with you at this meeting, at least form the habit of one person calling him each month on the day of the club meeting. Ask for late information on the club's portfolio and stocks being considered.

   At one time brokerage houses considered investment club transactions annoying. Now most firms welcome the business. For one reason clubs do grow into good-sized accounts, with steady monthly commissions. Brokers also find worthwhile fringe benefits when club members invest on their own. Figures prove that when most clubs start, only two of the members have their own investment accounts at a brokerage house. But in five years most members invest outside the club, choosing, often enough, the broker with whom the club does business.

2. Elect a presiding partner and other officers.
3. Decide on the amount per month each member will invest, usually $10 or $20 a month.
4. Stress that the club must invest for the long haul.
5. Set up, with the help of the NAIC manual, rules for handling shares when a member withdraws. The club should insist on several months' notice when a member wants to get out and take his money with him. In that time the club's monthly investments might cover the shares of the one who wants to quit. Or members might put up extra money to buy out

the partner who wants to leave. Or the club could transfer shares of some stock it owns to the withdrawing member—enough to cover his share of the partnership. Any of these ways would bypass capital gains tax for the rest of the club.

6. Explain that each member buys, not individual corporation shares, but a share of the partnership or investment club.

7. Ask for and vote on suggestions for a club name. The broker you deal with will open an account for the partnership name of your club, and place buy and sell orders for the club under its legal name. Some clubs conduct business in the "street" name, others keep their own certificates in a safety box.

8. Have each member sign the partnership form. Above all stress that the new club constitutes a legal partnership. No one sits back for a free ride. Each member takes her turn at holding office, serving on committees. Each partner keeps her eyes and ears open for every bit of information, in papers and magazines, on the air, relating to the corporations the club is evaluating.

    One successful club lists important sources of market information, such as Standard and Poor's reports, *Financial World, Forbes, Barrons, New York Times, The Wall Street Journal.* Each member is responsible for one source on the list. She either subscribes to the periodical or goes to the library and reads it in preparation for the monthly meeting.

9. Appoint two members to each prepare a study on a corporation to present to the club at the next meeting.

10. Coffee!

HELP FROM NAIC

1. *Investment Club Manual* covers the organization and operation of an investment club. The price may be deducted from your club's first year dues of $10. The manual contains a sample partnership agreement, a sample broker-club agreement, and instructions for keeping the books. The major part of the manual is devoted to illustrating and explaining stock study tools and procedures. These become the basis of the club's monthly meeting and the way members learn better investing techniques.
2. Monthly magazine *Better Investing* contains articles by financial counselors on various industries and corporations, and portfolio criticism of actual clubs, besides other helps.
3. Numerous charts and record-keeping helps can be bought, such as for stock selection and portfolio management.
4. NAIC provides tax and legal information, even seminars and classes in certain cities.
5. Each club paying the $10 annual membership fee gets a $25,000 fidelity bond covering the club.
6. Accounting service offers an investment club accounting manual and a monthly accounting service, for a fee, of course.

CLUB OFFICERS

Chairman or *presiding partner* serves for at least one year. She presides at monthly meetings, appoints committees, sets the time and place of the next meeting, and generally supervises the club.

Assistant presiding partner takes over in the absence of the chairman, supervises the Investment committee and the Portfolio Management committee.

Recording partner keeps the minutes and notifies members of meetings, absentees of action taken at meetings.

Financial partner keeps the club's financial records, including total invested in the club and the current value of each member's share. She issues a monthly statement to the club and an annual statement to each member for tax purposes. The partnership also files an annual tax return. The financial partner places buy and sell orders with the club's broker.

Because of the nature of this job, the woman in the club most capable with figures might well take the job indefinitely, and so be excused from the stock investigation committee. Be sure she has an understudy. One club found itself in trouble when its efficient and long-term financial partner quit because of serious illness and left no assistant.

As a matter of good business, insist on an annual audit of club books.

COMMITTEES

An *Investment committee,* used by some clubs, consists of a chairman and three or four members who serve for three or four months. Then the chairman appoints a new committee. In this way every member of the club serves on the Investment committee once a year. The committee investigates and evaluates several growth stocks each month. These companies may be slected by members of the club or by the Investment committee. Most successful clubs use some stock comparison form to evaluate stocks. NAIC sells a detailed one, highly effective, which requires homework to complete. Some brokerage houses provide their investment club accounts with a form, or you may draw up your own. Include such information as sales, dividends, earnings, and price.

The Investment committee reports on these stocks at each meeting. Limit each report to 10 minutes, allowing time afterward for club discussion of the stocks. After discussion the club votes either to buy shares of one of the stocks reported on, buy more shares of a stock it already holds, or wait another month to buy.

The *Portfolio Management committee,* appointed for a full year's service, reports every month on the standing of each stock in the club's portfolio. It may even recommend selling a stock that does not live up to NAIC requirements for successful investing.

The *Membership committee* searches out good replacements when a member quits the club.

Pitfalls lurk, of course, when a club begins. At first persuasive and vocal members tend to sway the others. For this reason, insisting that each member work on a committee and at some time hold each office in the club strengthens less aggressive members. Often less talkative women, when given opportunity, contribute clear-headed thinking. Similarly, conservative women can bring over-enthusiastic members down to earth. A level-headed woman will turn thumbs down on the club's choosing to invest in very speculative stocks, and will insist on thorough investigation of any company she puts her money into.

Because of pooled knowledge and viewpoints, most investment clubs rely less on a broker's advice than many individuals do. Nonetheless, it's important to have a good relationship with your broker. The first few years a club operates, though, are not very profitable ones for a broker—a small commission once a month, and if in street name, dozens of dividend statements and annual reports mailed to members.

Most clubs, however, register their stocks in their partnership name and use the address of one of the partners. Corporations mail financial reports and dividends directly to that person. Try to have all queries to the broker made by one person, by telephone as much as possible, or if at the broker's office, after the market closes.

NAIC FORMULA

The crux of the success of National Association of Investment Clubs is the four-point formula laid down by the Association.

1. *Invest regularly*, regardless of the fluctuations of the market. it takes fortitude to continue investing your $10 or $20 a month when the market is in a decline, but this is how shares are bought for lower prices.

2. *Reinvest* all earnings to compound income. Reinvesting dividends and capital gains for stocks sold adds, over a period of time, 4 to 6 percent to the club's portfolio growth rate.

3. *Diversify* by investing in different industries and different companies.

4. *Invest in growth stocks.* NAIC puts heavy emphasis on investing in growth stocks. What does the Association mean by a growth stock? Several famous growth stocks of outstanding past and continuing performance come to mind, but though these and others like them doubtless have years of growth ahead, NAIC cautions that they should only be bought when the price is favorable. Not the actual price per share, but the price in relationship to present and future earnings. Investors scramble for growth stocks, and popular opinion runs up the price, so that it sells for a high multiple of what the company earns on a share. The trick is to buy shares at the begin of the climb.

    Simply stated, a growth stock is one that grows faster than the economy as a whole. (You may recall that by economy we mean the circular flow of all goods and services produced in the United States and the money earned and spent for such.) In the latter part of 1968 the growth of our country's economy accelerated to an annual rate of 4½ percent. Whatever stocks your club invests in must show promise of much higher gain.

MINIMUM STANDARDS OF NAIC

The NAIC manual sets forth the minimum requirement for successful investing as buying stocks growing at the rate of at least 10 percent a year. This rate includes dividends not spent but reinvested, plus the increased value of your shares.

The test is growth in sales and earnings per share, coupled with increased dividends over the years. Here is where careful homework by all partners pays off. If six stocks meet the 10 percent annual growth test, and the club buys a seventh stock that fails the test, the club's whole average drags down.

In analyzing a stock for growth, clubs should check the company for at least a five-year period. If the company fails to pass the growth test in sales, earnings, and dividends, the stock should be rejected. It's a good idea, though, to hold such analyses for later appraisal, in the event the company may then meet the NAIC standard.

Most growth companies offer low dividends, or yield. Some companies pay none at all. Instead, most of its earnings are put back into the company for expansion. Over the years, though, a growth company not only increases sales and earnings, it usually increases its dividends. Some investment clubs pay attention to good dividends; others disregard this feature and look for gains in sales and earnings only.

INVESTIGATE THOROUGHLY

A growth stock must possess unusual earning power and good prospects for such earnings in the future. To find growth stocks with such prospects, the Investment committee will:

Compare sales, earnings, dividends for at least a five-year period.

Write for annual reports and other information on each company considered. Compare other companies in the same business.

NAIC also recommends that a club strive for the following division of invested money:

> 25 percent in smaller growth stocks
> 25 percent in major growth companies
> 50 percent in companies in between

When voting on whether to buy, hold or sell a stock, the majority rules. What happened before the decision should be past history. Losers keep still. One girl responsible for a certain stock in her club left on a six-month vacation. In the meantime the club voted to sell the stock. When the girl returned, she exclaimed, "You sold my stock!" But after that outburst she considered the matter closed.

Many clubs hold an anniversary dinner, a social time of getting to know each other better, a change from the regular business meeting.

Don't let investment club reports of easy gains fool you. Don't let hard work deter you. Hard work hovers over any club that increases its capital. It takes zing to run a successful club. About the only easy thing today is sliding downhill, and that's not even so easy as it once was!

Because each member brings her own viewpoint and special knowledge or skill to the club partnership, a club often out-performs what one person could do on her own. It is this combined knowledge and investing in several different stocks, thoroughly investigated, that enable investment clubs to make remarkable gains. Successful clubs emphasize an enterprising policy. They turn their backs on out-and-out speculation.

As in any other activity, results depend on what you put into the project. The harder each partner works to learn, the more your club will prosper. In addition, you can each apply what you learn to your own outside investment program.

To Benefit Most from This Chapter:

1. Send for NAIC *Investment Club Manual*
2. Talk to several women about starting an investment club.

How to Evaluate a Company 8

A junior-age boy I know made up a baseball-stock market game. The player spins an arrow for each pitch in the game. Whoever wins the inning sees his stock go up in value. Fine for a game, but that's no way for a woman to buy stocks. But I once heard of a woman who trusted to luck when she bought shares.

"I buy any stock that has 'great' in its name," she said. "That way I figure I can't lose."

Just as unthinking, hypothetical Mary Smith listened to tips and rumors in her office. Then she spent her lifetime savings on foreign gold stocks and other highly speculative issues. Mary Smith may see her shares go up in value. Much more likely, she will lose all she has.

Perhaps you would never trust to luck, or tips or rumors, but a haphazard approach can also cost you money. It's important to plan and study in order to be right about the stocks you choose to work for you. Nobody chooses a winner blindly.

Nor will a careful shopper buy a costly item on impulse. When a woman shops for a major household appliance or a new car, she plans ahead and shops around. If she's wise she compares prices, quality, brand names and listens to the sales pitch. The stove or car she buys must not only meet her need, but must be a good value as well. No woman really set on a certain brand of TV or electric typewriter will allow a salesman to talk her out of her choice.

HOW TO CHOOSE A WINNER

Similarly when it comes to buying stocks, you need to shop around, examine the company's financial reports, talk to the experts, then make your own selection. Never buy on the recommendation of a stranger, or even that of a well-meaning friend who likes to talk about the market, but has little knowledge of it. The advice of a businessman you know, who has investigated a stock, should be worth taking. Don't be taken in by *anyone*—stranger, friend, or relative—who urges you to buy a stock immediately, that if you don't the market will go up. Stocks should never be bought in haste (except by in-and-out traders who depend on timing, who also have more experience in the market than a beginner, and who frequently repent at leisure). Even your broker should not pressure you into a quick decision. A dependable broker will offer you one or two choices and give you time to think about the stock before you make your decision.

The stocks you buy need to be carefully planned for, then investigated and chosen because they fit your needs. You may not know much about computer leasing, conglomerates, or the mysteries of the laser beam, but any well-informed, intelligent woman can evaluate a corporation. If you can read a financial report and figure percentages, you can be your own expert.

LOOK AT YOUR NEIGHBORS

For a beginning why not investigate a local company or two, or a national corporation home-based in your vicinity? Fabulous Minnesota Mining (3M) started out in a small way in the city where I live. Most of my adult life I had heard tales of those who adventurously bought a few of Minnesota Mining's first shares and now were well-off and even wealthy. They had held onto those early shares through ups and downs with the company. Some employees even took their wages in shares of stock.

The spectacular growth of the company over past years is common knowledge. When I considered buying a few years back, I wanted to know if the company still possessed growth potential.

On the plus side, I knew several young businessmen who worked for and spoke highly of the company. Every time I used 3M products I thought, "This is great! What would I do without it?" I saw that the company advertised its creative new products nationally, that it built impressive, modern research plants, providing employment for many persons. Local newspapers carried an account of a nationwide program 3M instituted to help handicapped persons set up their own business. Then I read about the company's job training program.

As I studied the company's financial reports, I learned it had an excellent record of growth, increased sales, and earnings. All this added up to a sound growth company, attuned to social needs, and with a promising future.

My first shares of 3M, bought in 1966, have a cost base of $69. Later I bought shares for $78 and still later at $81. Toward the close of 1968 3M shares sold for $112, truly a fine growth stock.

You may not find a similar growth company nearby, but start right now to shop for the stock that will best fit your needs and work for you in the years ahead. Evaluate companies whose products you use in your home. Read the business page of your paper for news of local firms whose stock trades on exchanges or over-the-counter. Perhaps now would be a good time to review Chapter 3, Where to Get Help. Think while tossing the clothes into the dryer. You may even get in on the beginning of another giant growth company. Bigness, though, is not the only test of a growth company, as we'll see later.

INVEST FOR THE LONG HAUL

If you are a first-time investor, don't hop in and out of the market, trying to make quick profits. Choose stocks you intend to keep for at least ten years, or until circumstances alter the company's profits or your needs. Experts agree that the short-term investor does not succeed as well over the years as the long-term investor who chooses her stocks intelligently.

Turn your back on highly speculative stocks. Speculation tempts some beginners, who buy with the idea of holding the stocks until they go up and then selling at a profit. True, speculation may be an escalator to financial success for the woman who can afford to take risks with her money. Many have made substantial gains in this way, or even small fortunes. But countless others have lost small amounts to seven-figure fortunes with crashing suddenness.

Don't buy on margin, which means paying only part of the price and borrowing the rest from your broker. In the event of a market drop, the margin buyer must sell part of her stocks to cover the balance owed.

The woman who needs income must search for high-grade stocks with high dividends or yield. On the other hand, the woman who hopes to acquire future capital is better off investing in stocks that pay out little in dividends now, but have growth potential.

INVEST IN GROWTH STOCKS

By now you probably understand the four broad categories of common stocks:

Income (high dividends, but not much price increase)
Cyclical (tend to rise and fall with demand for the product or industry)
Speculative (new, experimental, or even risky)
Growth (earnings and sales growing faster than the economy)

Let's look at growth stocks, for here we women have the best opportunity to increase our capital—finding a winner.

WHAT DO THE EXPERTS MEAN WHEN THEY TALK ABOUT GROWTH STOCKS?

Certainly the stock should be in a growing industry. Some advisors look for future growth in such areas as oceanography, education and communications, drugs, and electronics. Others give the nod to industries that will benefit by the population increase, longevity, and full employment; for example, processed foods, utilities, and recreation products.

Because of the country's mounting population, nearly any industry that caters to consumers has some growth potential. But certain other features can help you spot a good growth company.

1. Increased sales and earnings

Some authorities call any firm a growth company whose sales increase at least 10 percent each year. Other specialists declare that labeling a corporation a growth company means its sales must be growing three times as fast as business, or the economy. At present this means nearly 14 percent a year.

Increased sales, of course, require more employees, larger plants, new outlay for equipment. In progressive companies more sales mean testing, planning, inventing new products in order to keep up with competition. As stated before, most growth companies put back into the company a large part of their earnings. In turn the price of the stock rises.

In addition, the stockholder also gets favorable tax treatment on deferred earnings. One stock may show increased earnings of 10 percent for the year and pay a 5 percent dividend, thus yielding a total of 15 percent. The stockholder reports the dividend as income (the first $100 in dividends is, of course, exempt from tax) and pays income tax on it.

Another stock may show a 14 percent growth rate in earnings and pay less than 1 percent dividends, thus calling for less current income tax. Of course, sometime in the future, you as stockholder must pay capital gains tax, but the tax on deferred earnings will probably be less because:

1 You may sell the stock after retirement when your income will be less than in your earning years.
2 Capital gains tax is half your regular income tax.

Investors in their earning years often search for low yield stocks.

With money for research and expansion a company stands to grow in sales and earnings. A note of warning: The company with the largest percentage sales increase does not always represent the best buy. Increased earnings are also important. Smaller companies may show a high percentage increase in sales and a correspondingly high increase in earnings. Those who know stress the importance of sales and earnings both increasing regularly.

A company about to offer its stock for public sale the first time may be a good buy. Take Dayton Corporation, Minneapolis, a solid local department store in business for many years. Its stock sold over-the-counter in the spring of 1967 for the first time at around $38 a share. Of course, hundreds of local investors who knew the company grabbed the first shares. Some brokers even carried waiting lists. After the initial flurry, the shares could be bought easily at $43 a share. A year and a half later Dayton's stock sold for $78, about an 81 percent increase, a fine gain for those early investors.

2. Increased price

Increased sales and earnings sooner or later hoist the price per share. What giant money-maker Sears Roebuck underscored in a note to stockholders is true of many other blue chip growth stocks. In 1931 Sears' stock sold for about $33. Today, after market appreciation, stock splits, and stock dividends, that one share has grown to $1,375.

DON'T BE ENTICED BY LOW PRICE

While we're talking about price, let's look at one mistake some women make in buying their first stocks—choosing the lowest priced ones they can find. They argue that they get more shares of a $2 stock for their money than of a $70 stock. They assume that the $2 stock will rise to $22 a share quicker than the $70 stock to $90. More often than not the low-priced stock is highly speculative, while many quality or blue chip stocks sell in the $50 to $75 price range. Though some "dollar" stocks have turned into outstanding growth stocks, countless others end up as market dropouts. Look for good value, not low price.

Look for companies whose sales and earnings (including dividends if any) both grow year after year at the rate of at least 10 percent a year. The trick is to discover these firms before 26 million other stockholders in the United States do. When a lot of people latch onto a beginning growth company they start a stampede for the stock and run it up in price like a flag on a pole. Learning that the institutions are buying large blocks of a stock you are interested in can also tip you off to the growth possibilities of that company. Financial page stock articles report large blocks of stock sold in various companies, an indication of institutional buying.

If you remember your homework, the price of a share of stock depends on two major factors: Earnings and public opinion. Since public opinion is usually unpredictable, the best way to judge a growth stock is not by the way its price goes up or down, but by the amount of money the company earns on each share of stock. Suppose you have narrowed your choice to:

Company A, whose stock rose 28 points last year, but whose earnings dropped 30 cents a share.

Company B, whose stock went up only 10 points in the same period, but showed earnings of 56 cents a share more than the previous year.

Choose Company B as the better growth company.

FASHIONS IN STOCKS

Fashions in stocks as well as in dresses run in cycles. In the

1920s, stocks with high income held the spotlight. After the market crash of 1929 cyclical stocks enjoyed popularity. (Those that depend on business or seasonal cycles.) Since World War II growth stocks have come into prominence, with the emphasis in the last decade on performance. Though fashions in stocks change, our aim should remain steady—to invest in stocks that increase in value.

We hear a lot about investing in performance stocks, well-managed stocks, to protect our money. The big question is: How do we spot well-managed stocks? How do we know the stock we are considering is more than a "glamor" stock or more than a fad?

3. Good management

One successful investor states that spotting good management holds first place in his appraisal of growth stocks. Another authority claims that management is 90 percent of his total evaluation.

It's almost elementary that good management turns out bigger gains in sales and earnings and wider profit margins than less competently managed firms. But how does a beginning investor learn whether the company she is considering is competently managed? Chiefly by reading, observing, studying, talking to others, especially her broker. (Brokerage firms call on their research teams to evaluate management of hundreds of companies.)

Ask yourself whether the management provides a favorable atmosphere for new product development. Examining the company's annual report will give some clues to this. As suggested before, you'll have a better opportunity to learn about management by considering companies located in your vicinity, since you may be able to talk to their employees.

Is management over-age? Usually the annual report prints a picture of the president, sometimes of other officers and directors. If all the officers are near retirement age, is the company training replacements? Financial magazines often print articles on top management, together with pertinent information.

If all officers and directors are scarely out of graduate school, do they know what they are doing? Here again a good financial magazine or paper can turn up some worthwhile answers.

Not long ago a national columnist wrote of a friend's method for judging management. After thoroughly studying a company's financial report, the man goes to the office and asks to meet the top executives and their assistants. He does this to observe how these men *dress.* Amusing, you say? Perhaps, but the man who follows this method is shrewd enough to know that clothes often reveal a rigid or progressive spirit. The man, by the way, has had outstanding success with his investments.[1]

What about the salaries of top executives? You'll find these reported in the company's prospectus. Do they compare favorably with salaries in like companies? Corporations are not above enticing competent management away from their competitors. Sometimes all it takes is a higher salary, pension and stock option plans. To retain creative top executives, corporations must pay salaries equal to or higher than their competitors pay.

How many shares of stock does the management team own? For management to own a large proportion of outstanding shares is probably evidence of good faith in the company. If most of the shares, though, are held by one family, it may be evidence of a tight corporation, too hide-bound for progress.

What sort of labor relations does the company have? Management has a lot to do with this.

Is the management alert to changing conditions, people's needs and ability to buy new products?

[1] Sydney Harris, "Strictly Personal," St. Paul Pioneer Press, December 8, 1968. (©Publishers-Hall Syndicate.)

What do competitive corporations think of your company's management?

In answering most of these questions your broker can be of great help. Results of their appraisal and research departments are yours for the asking.

You'll also want to check annual sales. Some giant growth companies show growth in sales of 5 to 7 percent a year. Such companies, well-known for their remarkable past growth, appeal to many new investors. But this is not enough to offset the rising economy. You need a stock that shows a 14 to 15 percent growth, including dividends.

Another indication of good management is a wide profit margin before taxes. (See Chapter 6, How to Read a Financial Report.) You divide a company's pretax profit by its sales to find the profit margin. One professional investor I talked to says that a profit margin of 10 percent on sales of 100 million is as good as a profit margin of 2 percent on sales of 500 million, and the growth is more likely to be better in the smaller company.

Still another indicator is to figure the earnings on invested capital. You divide the book value per share (See Chapter 6) into the earnings per share. Some experts say that when a company earns 10 percent to 25 percent on invested capital, good management is evident.

INVEST IN QUALITY

For a woman just beginning to invest, quality is of prime importance. In today's market we hear a lot about high-flying, "go-go" stocks. Though the temptation be great, never give up quality to make quick profits. You take too big a risk. Even diversification is no substitute for quality.

What do we mean by quality in a stock?

Standard and Poor's *Stock Guide* gives hundreds of stock ratings from A+ to C. Plainly stated though, a quality stock is a sound established company with:

How to Evaluate a Company

A long record of consecutive dividends
A long record of increased earnings and sales
A fairly wide profit margin
Management of integrity and progressiveness
An industry that is modern and has a future

After you have a firm foundation of quality stocks, or even before, if you have $1,000 you don't mind losing, you might want to buy a more or less speculative stock with good prospects. For instance:

1 The stock of a young company that shows increased earnings and sales over a period of three to five years.
2 A stock in a beginning industry that may climb in the future, possibly connected with space, oceanography, air freight.
3 A company offering its shares to the public for the first time, one likely to grow with the economy.

Remember, these should be stocks that you have thoroughly investigated.

For the beginner buying highly speculative stocks, hoping for the pot of gold, rarely fulfills a woman's dreams. But buying stock in an established company of proven worth with promising future prospects usually gives good results.

A study printed recently in newspapers reported that the top ten stocks most widely held in 1967 by the institutions showed a total profit of 25 percent. Had you bought one share of each of these ten stocks the first of 1967, totalling $1,071.56, eleven months later the shares would have been worth $1,341.58, or a gain of $270.02. This represents a gain of 25.2 percent for the period, not counting any dividends. The top ten stocks most widely held by the institutions included such quality stocks as IBM, General Electric, Texaco, Mobil Oil.

Another reason for choosing a high-grade stock with good sales and earnings over the years is that it probably will not drop far even if the market skids downward. Also, companies with quality stock accumulate surplus funds from which they may, in time of recession when earnings might be poor, continue to pay dividends to their stockholders.

PROTECT YOUR MONEY BY DIVERSIFICATION

One investment authority states that diversification cannot be overlooked if a woman wants to be a success as an investor. Perhaps you recall the various ways to diversify stock holdings.

1. Industries—oil, steel, electronics, banks. (Brokers list at least 29 categories.)
2. Companies—within a given industry, such as Standard Oil of New Jersey, Mobil Oil, Union Oil.
3. Sections of the country—south, mid-west, Alaska.
4. Period of time of investments.
5. Common stocks, preferred stocks, corporation bonds.

And getting down to fundamentals, before investing in stocks at all, you need insurance, government bonds, savings account.

The reason for not putting all your money in one stock is that should something fatal happen to your company, you would lose everything. But spread over several industries and companies such loss is less likely. Although to diversify your stock holdings is one of the tenets of successful investing, never sacrifice quality for the sake of variety.

Suppose you are just getting your feet wet as an investor and have $1,000 to invest. The best way to begin is by buying shares in one established company. The next time you have saved enough to buy more shares, you choose a company in a different industry. With a larger sum to invest, you would, in order to diversify your holdings, buy shares in several companies in as many industries. For further diversification you should spread the money over a period of time. The additional amount paid in commissions would add little to the total cost.

Suppose you have $5,000 to invest. You have thoroughly investigated Economics Laboratories, General Electric Company, Johns-Manville, Union Carbide, F.W. Woolworth Company. Choose one of the companies and buy $1,000 worth of shares, or a little less. A month or two later buy shares in another of the companies, and so on. This way you will have not only spread your money over five different industries, but you will have bought at diverse market conditions, up or down from when you bought the first shares.

Should you choose a rather new, smaller company, with good growth prospects, you should diversify even more, by dividing the $1,000 you have to invest and putting part of it in a similar but more established company. Never buy stock of a company so new you have no way of checking it.

When, after investing your $5,000, the time comes when you want to buy more shares, choose one of the companies in which you already own stock and buy more shares. Be sure the shares are not overpriced, that is, at an all-time high. Check this in the weekly quotation page of your newspaper, which reports the high and low prices for the year thus far.

For a time five companies will be enough for you to watch. For a $10,000 portfolio you might work toward eight or ten stocks in as many industries. When you can invest more money, you probably will be wiser to buy more of the good stocks you have, unless they are overpriced at the time, than to branch out into more companies than you can conveniently watch.

Whenever you study and investigate a stock, keep your findings on file. Later you may discover that one of the stocks you didn't buy turns up a better record of sales and earnings than the one you bought, and therefore may be a good addition or replacement to your portfolio.

INVEST REGULARLY

The principle of regular investing is the basis for a sound financial program. This is one of the standards of The

National Association of Investment Clubs (See Chapter 7). The New York Stock Exchange bases its Monthly Investment Plan (MIP) on regular investment. The great appeal of mutual funds comes from the discipline of regular investment. Women who succeed in the stock market usually buy a certain amount of good quality stock regularly.

TIMING

Try not to buy stocks at all-time high prices. Most stocks fluctuate throughout the year, some on a definite pattern. Try to discover this.

REVIEW YOUR HOLDINGS

Unlike marriage, when you buy stocks you don't promise to stay together "until death do us part." Some women, though, persist in such attachment to their stocks. Stashed away in safety boxes lie certificates for stocks no longer growing. Some companies have even cut dividends. To avert such a sad state, you should not only evaluate your investment program at least once a year, but constantly keep watch over it. Ask yourself about each stock:

Is it still good quality?
Does it pay regular dividends?
Have sales and earnings increased at least 10 percent the past year?
Is the price per share rising?
What is the profit margin?

Even after taking the best precautions, a woman may find that a chosen stock is at a standstill, or worse yet, on a down slide. Changes in business, the government, the economy, tax rulings—all occur frequently and can affect your holdings. Or some internal problem or laxness may be the offender. Likewise, your own needs may impel you to change your investments.

PROFESSIONAL YARDSTICK

I have found excellent help from the portfolio appraisal service Merrill Lynch offers all its accounts. Other brokerage houses do the same. Toward the end of the year, but in time to make any tax-benefit changes, I hand my broker a list of the stocks I own, including the name of the company, number of shares, whether common or preferred. With this I enclose a short statement of the purpose of my investment program—to protect and increase my capital, to move some of my holdings for gifts to minors and the church. Another woman might stress avoiding income now and pushing for increased capital in the future. Still another might wish to change from growth stocks to high income stocks.

With such information at hand, a highly skilled research team in the head office examines my portfolio. Back comes a detailed appraisal with the recommendation to sell a stock or two. The appraiser usually suggests two or three replacements, and to help me make the choice sends resume sheets on these companies.

Admittedly I have not always followed the advice offered. In some instances I gained by holding what I had. In one case I waited too long to sell a certain stock and so lost out on a substantial capital gain. I acquired respect for the firm's New York research department.

Even though you bought your stocks after careful investigation, not all will perform alike. Some may skyrocket, others will climb leisurely. Some may even settle down for a long winter's nap. Your job is to determine whether such sluggishness is temporary or a pattern of future behavior. You do this by constant watch over your holdings, weeding out disappointments and substituting winners. If your study convinces you one of your companies has entered a decline, the stock should be sold immediately and another bought that will work for you. Keep in mind that even though the market as a whole may be advancing, some of your stocks may be losing ground. Replace them.

WHEN TO SELL

The success of any woman's investment program depends not only on knowing what to buy and when to buy it, but on when to sell. Most experts agree that bad actors should be sold for good replacements. Many beginners hold quite the opposite view. They sell their outstanding performers, taking the profits, and hold onto the stocks that show losses. Or even more fatal, they sell quality stocks because they need money.

How do you develop the ability to spot a poor performer? It's just the reverse of choosing a good quality stock. If quarterly reports show a drop in earnings, investigate further. If the price per share has dropped steadily, investigate. You may discover pointers that tell you to hold the stock, such as high expenses for unusual research. Again your investigation may show the company is not meeting its competition, or that new and less capable management has taken over. A drop in the price-earnings ratio is special cause for concern. If facts and figures prove the stock is not fulfilling its promise for growth, then begin to sell, spreading the total over several months.

This technique paid off for me when I sold shares of a glamor stock in three parts. Brokers advised me to unload all my shares at once. My own investigation proved that earnings had skidded to an all-time low. I sold the first shares at $60 a share. Six months later I sold the second batch at $90. A year later I sold more shares for $142, replacing them each time with quality stocks. Though the public continues to scramble for the stock I sold, the large number of shares I held was too risky for my purposes.

When it comes to selling, however, you should guard against being influenced by rumors. Selling on a rumor is as foolish as buying on a rumor. Investors sold stock in a particular corporation on reports that the company lost its best officers to competition. Later the stock soared to double its price because stockholders had confidence in the new management.

How to Evaluate a Company

Investing in common stocks needs to be carefully weighed. On one side of the scale is the well-known fact that investing in stocks is riskier than putting your money in U.S. government bonds. Investing in stocks holds more risk than putting your money in the bank. It may even be riskier than hiding your cash under the mattress.

On the other side of the scale, putting your money where it does not grow along with the economy, or at least at the rate of 10 to 14 percent a year, compounded, is also risky. In the end you may find yourself with fixed dollars, money that buys less and less each year.

Of course, blue chip or quality stocks can go down in value. They often have in the past, but over the years the trend has been steadily upward. Of 1,206 common stock issues listed in 1967 on the New York Stock Exchange, 1,038 went up for the year, 903 of them 10 percent and more, while only 162 stocks went down. It should not be too difficult to find a winner.

Our country has been in a long period of prosperity, resulting in upward prices in the stock market. Any number of conditions can bring about a change in the stock market and send it plunging down for a short or long period. You must harden yourself to withstand such market drops.

HOW DO YOU FIND A WINNER?

Not by any bag of tricks, but by tools of the trade do you choose winners.

1. Be skeptical. Study facts, figures and the economy.
2. Check stock ratings. Compare high and low prices and earnings of corporations.
3. Talk to company employees.
4. Seek the opinion of experts.
5. Invest for the long term.

Many people spend most of their time earning money and only a very small percentage of time working to invest it. But money properly invested after careful investigation can bring in many times the amount a woman could earn in the same length of time. A young investor I know told me that last year he made paper profits of $10,000 on an investment which began about ten years ago in a very modest way. This was a fine addition to his salary, with about an hour's work a week spent on the project.

If a young family man, with a full-time job can profitably oversee his investments, why can't women? Older women especially, who are left with more or less fixed income, might spend time trying to increase it by informed investing.

You may not agree with Aristotle's observation that success is better when it's difficult to achieve, but *your* success as an investor will certainly be better the harder you work at it.

In the years since I first started investing I learned that just about all that can be written about the stock market, all anybody knows about it, is either history or forecasting. Since no one has ever proved the ability of soothsayers, I'd rather bank on *hard work*.

The woman who thoroughly investigates her stocks, investing in high quality stocks for the long haul, who invests regularly, reviews her portfolio periodically, weeds out poor performers and holds onto good stocks through ups and downs of the market, will find she manages a sound investment program. When she adds up the results at the end of the year, she is bound to find she has winners.

To Benefit Most from This Chapter:
1. Settle on your own needs or goals. Do you want high income now? Or would deferred income now and greater growth in the value of your shares suit your purpose better?
2. Select three or four corporations home-based, or with branch offices in your vicinity. Evaluate their products or services. Talk to employees about the company. Try to learn what the management is like.
3. Narrow your choice to the most favorable stock.

Final Check-Up Before You Buy   9

Homework finished? You've read and studied and learned all about the company you want to invest in and the industry as a whole? Then it's time to sit back, review, and answer a few questions.

MONEY TO INVEST

You've ear-marked a sum of money for investing. Of course, the money is what you have over and above your daily requirements, emergency account, and insurance payments. After so carefully choosing your stock and buying it, you'd hate to have to sell it hurriedly. Whether you sold in a rising market and so couldn't wait for the full profits, or in a depressed market with lower prices, you'd lose either way.

LONG-RANGE PLAN

Success in any undertaking requires a plan. Investing in the stock market is no exception. Your plan might include regular investments, working toward a set amount of capital invested, protection of your capital, and a hedge against inflation.

Your investment plan might also provide for a certain percentage of your capital to be invested in different types of stocks. For example, as time goes on, you invest 15 percent in government bonds, 75 percent in quality stocks with growth potential, and 10 percent in more speculative growth companies. You should, though, leave the more speculative stocks until you build up your capital in quality stocks.

By choosing your investments according to a long-range plan, you are more than likely to protect and increase your money.

QUESTIONS TO ASK YOURSELF

You have evaluated at least three stocks, in the same industry since right now you expect to buy just one stock. You can find a good investment opportunity any time, but you want a top-notch one.

Where does the company you are interested in stand on the ladder of success? Is it the top company in the industry, a large, well-established profit-maker? Or is it a fair to middling sized company, sound and with steady profits? Or is it a new company, say less than three years old, small, struggling, but with keen, imaginative management?

The first two stand out as better investment choices for the beginner. The new struggling company, riskier than the other two, might be taken on after you own half a dozen quality stocks.

What about prospects for growth in the industry as a whole? Does the company manufacture a product that people couldn't do without some years back, but now a better product has usurped its place? For instance, hairpins and hair spray, black and white TV and color TV.

What about future sales volume? Are you counting on a steady increase in sales for a product that people buy when they have money, but would turn their backs on in time of a recession? In the case of a company that manufactures pleasure boats, snowmobiles, or other luxury items exclusively, sales and earnings may drop in a bear market.

From a practical standpoint you need to answer such questions before you buy.

Final Check-Up Before You Buy

CHOOSE A LISTED STOCK

Over-the-counter stocks, though offering attractive bargains, are not as strictly regulated as those on the exchanges, though speculative stocks are listed there, too. The American Stock Exchange lists more speculative stocks, and trading is more speculative than on the New York Stock Exchange. Of course, high quality stocks are to be found among over-the-counter issues as well as on the AMEX and NYSE. But listed stocks, as a rule, prove safer investments for the beginner.

IS THE PRICE RIGHT?

One way to tell if a stock is priced too high is to compare the price-earnings ratio of the stock for several years. (Price of one share of stock divided by annual earnings per share.) Standard and Poor's *Stock Guide* reports the price-earnings ratio on more than 4,500 stocks. For comparison of previous years consult Standard and Poor's *Statistical Reports* in the library or brokerage office.

Some years ago, authorities considered a price-earnings ratio of 10 or 11 or 12 about right. If a stock sold for $48 and earned $4.20 a year per share, the price-earnings ratio was 11, or 11 to 1. In other words, the stock cost 11 times as much as it earned.

Most experts today hesitate to set a dogmatic rule about price-earnings ratio—what is too high, what is too low. Shrewd investors try to catch a stock about to take off. If you buy a stock with a P/E ratio of 15 and the company's sales and earnings increase so that the P/E ratio reaches 30 times earnings, good for you. But if you buy that same stock at 30 times earnings, you may get in on the small end of the company's growth.

In 1961, when the Dow Jones industrial average hit 735, the P/E ratio of the 30 stocks rose to 23. At the close of 1968 the Dow Jones industrials showed a P/E ratio of 16 to 1. Here are the price-earnings ratios of a few high-grade stocks as reported in Standard and Poor's *Stock Guide* for September, 1968:

American Home Products	27
Owens-Corning Fiber Glass	32
Simplicity Pattern Company	39
Upjohn Company	20

To buy when the P/E ratio is at its low and sell when at the high would be a neat trick if you could bring it off. What a woman needs to learn is whether such high price-earnings ratios represent a continuing pattern of increased sales and earnings or whether the figures mean that public opinion and high institutional buying have boosted the price of the stock so that it is overpriced.

One analyst suggests that a price-earnings ratio of 14 is moderate enough today, other conditions being favorable, to make a stock worthy of investment. It helps to have a bargain instinct that recognizes undervalued issues.

TIMING

If you keep a hypothetical portfolio as suggested in Chapter 2, Use a Trial Portfolio, you already know that the prices of most stocks fluctuate. Any annual quotation of stock prices gives a price range between the high and the low for the period. You will note that many stocks fluctuate 10 or 15 percent in the year, some as much as 30 percent.

Suppose, after investigation, you decide you want RCA stock in your actual portfolio. You have watched it for some time now. The newspaper quotations show that so far this year RCA sold at a high of 55 and a low of 44 ¼. Twenty shares at $55 equals $1,100. Twenty shares at $44.25 would cost only $885, a savings of $215 (not counting commissions and other charges).

Now no one will guarantee that RCA shares will again sell for $44.25 in the coming months, but it will pay you to check prices for the past few years to learn if a pattern of up and down price exists. Possibly by waiting a month or two you can time your purchase to get in on the lower share price. Don't wait so long, though, that you pay a higher price than you might have by investing earlier. Even if you buy at the stock's high price for the past few years, if you are sure the stock is one you want, that it has growth promise, go ahead. If the stock does well, you may one day laugh at the *low* price you paid. If it goes up 10 points in the next two months after you buy, you will make $200 in paper profits.

The reason for buying shares in any company is that after careful study you believe the company has good prospects for growth and that the present market price is right for you to buy.

The other side of timing is in-and-out trading, which you should firmly resist.

AVOID PROCRASTINATION

Once you reach a decision to buy or sell, never procrastinate. Painful results can easily follow, as I learned to my sorrow when I put off selling some stock a few years ago.

Though my broker advised me late one November to sell a stock because of poor earnings and other difficulties, I waited six months to sell. First, I argued blithely, I would let the month of December go by because I had already sold other stock that year with a high capital gain. After the first of the year I would sell.

Bogged down with work and pleasure I let half the month of January go by before I realized the stock had gone into a tailspin. From $120 a share at the time the broker advised selling, the stock skidded to $77 a share. Next I thought surely I ought to wait until the shares went up again before selling. Altogether I hung onto the stock six months while it sagged and then stood still. All wrong decisions, made by a beginner. Had I not procrastinated I would have been several hundred dollars ahead. All the while my money could have been invested in worthwhile stock and working for me.

On the other hand, prompt action paid off a while back when I bought Westinghouse Electric at 51 and saw it climb to 77 in less than a year's time.

CHOOSE A BROKER AND OPEN AN ACCOUNT

If you have not already done so, visit the office of a nationally known brokerage house, with branch offices in most cities of size. If you live in a small town you may have to deal with your banker or drive to a nearby city. Tell the account executive your financial situation, your objectives, how much you plan to invest, and the stock you want to buy.

Should the broker (account executive) recommend other stocks than the one you have selected, be sure you understand why. It's your money. But don't forget he's the expert. He can put his hand on numerous research facts and figures that enable him to appraise a stock. His ear is attuned to the market. But don't expect him to guarantee any stock he approves or recommends. He simply can't.

Suppose your broker agrees with the wisdom of your choice. He may reply, "You want to buy 20 shares of RCA at the market." This means that his firm's broker on the floor of the NYSE will enter into an auction with another broker to obtain the best price for you. The local broker will route your buy order to the firm's NYSE odd-lot broker. In turn he will head for the trading post where brokers trade RCA stock and begin the two-way auction, each broker seeking to obtain the best price for his customer.

After the New York broker buys the stock, he relays the information to your account executive, who will charge your account for the amount. Later the office mails you a confirmation slip with all details of the transaction, including your account representative's commission and any tax. An odd-lot sale costs more proportionately than a sale for 100 shares. You must send your payment for the shares to the brokerage office within five days of the actual sale.

UNSCRUPULOUS BROKERS

Taking care of your money begins with the advice you receive and follow on investments. As far as I know I have never met a dishonest broker, but no one can deny they exist. Columnists who write about investing often use illustrations of dishonest brokers. The papers carry tales of untrained, inexperienced investment staffs who set themselves up as "security advisors," and put out "advisory" letters, for a fee. Brokerage houses have sometimes come under SEC investigation, resulting in warnings or punishments.

With the human heart what it is, with present-day attitudes toward right and wrong what they are, you may come into contact with wheeling and dealing, or dishonesty. If so, shop around until you find a broker you can trust. Don't be pushed into indiscriminate buying and selling.

SPREAD YOUR INVESTMENT

Most authorities advise that a woman with $4,000 or $5,000 to invest should spread the amount over a period of time, not invest it all at once. For example, she might buy 20 shares of a $40 stock she had carefully investigated. After watching its price for month or two and satisfied the stock was doing what she expected it to, she might buy another 20 shares. All the while she should keep watch for any news of the company, and even talk about it to others. If all goes well, she might buy another 20 shares. By that time she should switch to another company and another industry to build up diversification.

REGISTER YOUR STOCK

Some husbands and wives register all their certificates in joint tenancy. If one person dies the stock will belong to the other without going through probate. (See Chapter 14, What to Do About Your Income Tax, for a discussion of this.) Others register some stock in the husband's name, some in the wife's. As a single woman you will use your own name, unless you choose to leave your shares in street name. (See Chapter 12, Keeping Essential Records.)

YOU MIGHT TRY A FORMULA

You can't read very much about stock market investing before you come across formulas—intended to help you beat the market. One formula that people talk a lot about is "buy low, sell high, buy back low." You won't find any how-to advice for such a formula in this book. Some investors, though, buy stocks by such methods as charts, computer analysis, and even far-fetched dreams. Others depend on mathematical computations, theories, and other tactics.

1. Mathematical plan

In his book *Understanding Stocks,* Don Campbell explains one mathematical formula. You write yourself a note, I assume, or at least make yourself a deal, that whenever the stock you buy goes down a certain number of points, you will sell all of it and take a loss. Whenever your stock goes up the same certain number of points, you will sell a certain percentage of its total value, say 10 percent. You also set a high figure at which, if the stock goes that high, you will sell all the shares you own of that stock. Here's how it works:[1]

> To get our plan into operation we have resolved that we will base our selling strictly on 8-point fluctuations in the stock's price. Now let us see what action we would take if the stock were to enjoy a run-up that, admittedly may not be typical, but that illustrates our plan in operation quite graphically (remember, we have started with 100 shares purchased at $20 a share and that, subsequently, the stock has gone to the following levels):

---

[1] From UNDERSTANDING STOCKS, By Don Campbell. Copyright © 1965 by U.S. Industries, Inc. Reprinted by permission of Doubleday & Company, Inc.

Final Check-Up Before You Buy

28	sell 10 shares	$280
36	sell 10 shares	360
44	sell 10 shares	440
52	sell 10 shares	520
58	sell 10 shares	580
50	sell 50 shares	2,500
		$4,680

This takes will power, but the writer claims the mechanical formula pays off because you'll never lose more than 10 percent of what you paid for the stock and while the stock climbs you will steadily take your profits.

This formula is especially suited to the investor who either by lack of time or inclination fails to make a thorough investigation of the stock he buys.

2. Dow theory

Another prescription for investing with success, the Dow theory, consists of market movements and signals by which Dow theorists insist they can forecast market changes and take advantage of them.

3. Dollar averaging

Invest the same amount of money in a certain stock at regular periods. Thus you buy more shares when the price is low and fewer shares when the price is high.

4. Averaging down

In averaging down, if you are satisfied that your stock is a good buy at $50 a share, you buy more shares when it goes down in price, so bringing down the average price per share.

5. Fixed amount

Decide on a fixed amount you want to keep invested at all times. Periodically when the value of your shares rises, sell enough shares to keep your investment constant and deposit the profits in your bank account. You must also have extra money in the bank to buy more shares in case the price of your shares drops below your fixed amount. Presumably your bank account will in time grow and you will buy additional stocks.

6. Fixed percentage

Plan what percentage of your capital will be in stocks and what percentage in the bank. When the market value of your stocks goes up above that percentage, sell enough to bring it back down. When the market value of your stocks drops below the fixed percentage, withdraw money from the bank to buy more stock and bring up the level. Presumably your bank account will grow from this method, too.

7. Diversify

Diversifying is a form of formula investing, spreading your investment among several companies, thus protecting yourself against losing all if, in a market plunge, your particular investment proved especially vulnerable.

Formulas, methods, recipes have worked well for different investors at different times. On the other hand, countless successful investors attest to the fact that the *principle* of investigating a company, holding its stock for years, or until it changes, is the way to protect and increase capital.

FINAL CHECK

Whether you follow a formula or a principle, you will recognize that risk is always possible in stock market investing. Before you buy, be sure you have not multiplied that risk by failing to observe any of the following proven rules:

1. Invest only after you have provided for daily needs, insurance, and emergencies.

Final Check-Up Before You Buy

2. As a beginner, invest only in reliable leading companies.
3. Never buy on intuition, tips or rumors.
4. Never buy under high pressure. If anyone tries to hurry you, sleep on your decision.
5. Choose a reliable brokerage firm to deal with and talk over your objectives with your account executive.
6. Don't be tempted into in-and-out trading.
7. Avoid other high risk situations—unlisted stocks, speculative stocks, buying on margin, and selling short.
8. Make up your own mind and don't allow yourself to be pressured into a course you haven't checked out.
9. Don't underestimate your skill as a woman investor.

Once I listened to a Paine, Webber, Jackson and Curtis account executive lecture on investing. She said, "Men move money more aggressively in and out of the market than women do." She illustrated by telling about one couple whose accounts she handled. The husband did a lot of in-and-out trading while his wife held onto her choices. Not surprisingly, over a period of years, the wife did better than her husband.

Ready to buy? Then buy! No need to panic if in the next few months your well-investigated stock fails to live up to your expectations or gives off a "no joy" signal. No need to bite your finger nails if the Dow Jones industrial average drops five points in one day. Remember that means the average blue chip stock in the DJI dropped only about 40 or 50 cents a share. Even if the market appears to be on a roller-coaster trend of big dips, keep steadfast in your opinion of the stock you so carefully chose. Don't be afraid to buy more shares at such a time. Some of the best bargains can be picked up in a down market.

Give your company a chance. You bought your shares for the long-term investment. Have the patience to wait to see what happens, not next Tuesday, but next year, or until something occurs to change your mind.

It all boils down to a woman investing on her own having know-why as well as know-how.

Should your stock soar instead of drop, rejoice. With confidence you can set aside other funds for investing. As soon as the amount is large enough, perhaps $500 or more, and you have investigated another company, buy more shares. The way to increase your capital is to regularly buy new shares. If possible reinvest your dividends to compound your gains.

Far more important than watching every dip and spurt of the market is watching the performance of the companies whose stock you buy. At first you'll need to spend an hour a day at a desk or at the library, studying, figuring, evaluating. But along with such work goes the mental work you tuck into every cranny of your day. Wonder as you work around the house, as you drive to the supermarket, as you wait for an appointment. Take advantage of every opportunity at work or in your home to talk about business, the economy, and investments to those who know. File every tidbit away in your subconscious, ready to be pulled out when needed.

Before you know it you're a stockholder, sharing in the success of American business, a far more enviable spot than that of the woman who basks in credit card castles.

To Benefit Most from This Chapter:

1. Select the company with the most favorable prospects from those you have evaluated.
2. Find the current price of the stock in your newspaper quotations. Pick up your checkbook and figure out how many shares you can buy. Don't forget the broker's commission.
3. Set off for the brokerage house and buy x number of shares!

What You Should Know About Trusts and Mutual Funds   10

Investment trusts and mutual funds do the work for you like a TV dinner from the frozen food counter. And whatever you think of TV dinners, they are a boon to busy people. Taking everything into consideration, they can give you good results, and so can the funds.

From a practical point of view the funds save you time. Instead of researching and investing in several corporations yourself and then overseeing each one, you invest in a fund.

A fund should also earn money for you. It takes your money and all that's received from its thousands, often millions, of investors and buys a wide variety of stocks. A fund buys and sells stock in order to earn money—for itself and its customers. If the stock does not grow in value and dividends, who will buy it?

Something else a good fund provides is top-flight management, including market analysts and shrewd counselors. Naturally it pays them salaries, or fees, comparable to top management in business. When you buy investment or mutual fund shares, the cost of management is included in the package.

Each investor then owns a small cut of the combined stock holdings of the fund. All capital gains (which come when the management sells fund shares at a profit) plus the dividends are distributed to each shareholder according to the number of shares owned. This amount is usually credited to the shareholder's account, but it can be withdrawn instead. (Some closed-end funds do retain dividends, paying their own income tax.)

The regular withdrawal plan many mutual funds advertise lured me. A woman can invest a minimum of $10,000 or agree to make regular payments toward that sum over a period of years. Then she can withdraw a stated amount or percentage monthly or quarterly.

There ended my knowledge of the subject at the time I bought my first mutual fund shares.

What I knew about mutual funds beckoned me, even though for some time I had successfully bought and sold various stocks. To my satisfaction the stocks my husband left me increased in value in the market drop of 1966. In that year the Dow Jones industrial average dropped 102 points or 11 percent.

Let me hasten to give credit to my husband's wisdom in selecting stocks. I remember the day the broker told us, "You have a great portfolio, a fine combination of blue chips, growth and speculative stocks. I wish all my customers had as good judgment as you."

My husband bought each stock because he believed the company to be well-managed with growth potential. A few, the speculative ones, when bought, had yet to prove their worth, but have since made impressive gains. Up to this point I have not bought speculative stocks. For a man with a salary in a solid position occasionally to buy a speculative stock is one thing. But for a woman dependent on income and safety to do so is something else. Working on one of my husband's principles, I have bought high-grade solid stocks that I hope to keep for a period of years, stocks that I expect to increase in value and dividends.

Another rule my husband believed in is that if a once good stock falls in value for some reason or fails to serve its purpose, it should be sold. On this basis I made several changes which proved to be successful.

SOMETHING LESS THAN SUCCESS

Pride goeth before a fall, resting on your laurels, inexperience, and all that combined to jolt me out of smugness when I invested in mutual funds. It makes no difference that I *thought* I was right.

One of the insurance policies left me paid over $100 a month for eight years. A fixed amount to count on for that period of time and then whoof!—it would end.

Not needing the $100 a month right then as much as I might later, I studied how to invest this amount every month to advantage. The target was not only to protect my capital, but to increase it to offset the dollar's nonstop plunge in buying power, the rising cost of living and higher taxes. Then at the end of eight years I could withdraw a monthly amount, leaving the capital intact.

Mutual funds sprang up as the answer. A salesman explained the system to me. To begin I could buy a certain number of shares, then pay $100 a month until the investment reached $10,000, the minimum under the plan. Any time afterward I could withdraw monthly payments of about 6 percent of the total value without digging into the capital. All the while my mutual fund shares would be piling up money for me. Sounds great. But it hasn't worked that way.

The salesman left the company prospectus and financial report for me to read. I read the fine print, scanned the list of corporations the mutual fund invests in. Some of them were the same ones I already owned. But diversification was wide, a talking point in the fund's favor. If the market dropped, perhaps not all the stocks the fund held would also drop. Supposedly the fund's shares would not drop as far as the market as a whole.

The fund was well-established, not a new unproven one, with a fine record of growth over the past ten years. It gave the choice of investing in its income fund, growth fund, speculative or balanced fund. Since I was more interested in increasing my capital than in income at the time, I chose the growth fund contract. A contract does not mean you will be held to it if something happens to prevent your making payments. You can always back out. Ah, but there the shoe pinches.

You might think that I would have investigated several mutual funds, but I didn't. The one before me looked good. Taking $5,000 capital I signed up to buy $10,000 worth of shares and agreed to pay $100 a month on the balance. If I missed a payment occasionally, the salesman assured me, I would not be penalized.

The pinch was that the salesman's commission for the entire $10,000 contract and the initial service charge for the fund's know-how subtracted a big chunk from my first investment. Commission and service charges amount to 8 ½ percent, the bulk of it taken out of my initial investment and the rest from monthly payments. This meant my initial $5,000 bought only $4,375.75 worth of shares. Of each monthly investment of $100 on the contract only $98.50 went to buy new shares. At the close of each year the mutual fund credited my account with dividends and capital gains distributions, less costs.

HERE IS HOW IT WORKED

		Paid to the fund	Actually Invested
Initial payment on contract		$5,000.00	
Salesman fee subtracted	$599.25		
Service fee	25.00		
Total	624.25		
Balance invested in shares			$4,375.75
Dividends paid first year		112.25	
Capital gains paid first year		105.50	
Total reinvested			217.75
12 monthly payments @ $100		1,200.00	
(Less service and sales charges)			1,082.00

What You Should Know About Trusts and Mutual Funds

	Paid to the Fund	Actually Invested
Dividends paid second year	140.44	
Capital gains paid second year	342.24	
Total reinvested		482.68
12 monthly payments @$100	1,200.00	
(Less service and sales charges)		1,082.00
Total	8,100.43	7,240.18
Net asset value of shares 2 years later	8.70	
Total value of shares 2 years later		7,663.13

The point is that after two years I had not yet recovered the amount of the sales fee and service charge. Critics and the Securities and Exchange Commission believe this fee should be spread over the entire period of investing. Certainly it should be picture-window clear that any woman who panicked and sold her mutual fund shares early in her contractual plan, or for some reason was unable to finish the contract, would lose out. (If a woman changes her mind within 30 days of signing the contract most funds will refund her money.)

Of course the market skidded into a low period in the two years. But had I left the money in the bank at 4 percent interest I would have been ahead. Time certificates would have paid over 5 percent making more than a $500 increase on the $5,000 alone. If I had put the money in IBM shares at $335 my capital would have increased to over $10,000 for the same period of time.

Despite all this looking in the rear-view mirror, I continue to invest in this fund because I believe it a good one. Completing the contract provides security—a fund from which I can withdraw regular payments. As since pointed out to me, there was no reason why, with a $5,000 initial investment, I should have entered into a contractual plan.

This was my experience. It need not be yours. Before you show the mutual fund salesman to the door, read on.

LOOK BEFORE YOU BUY

Because I was less than ardent about my investment in mutual funds I read a book or two on the subject. The terms *investment funds, investment trusts,* and *mutual funds* are sometimes used interchangeably. More often investment funds and investment trusts refer to closed-end funds, while mutual funds refer to open-end funds. This is the distinction made from now on. You'll find prices for both these quoted on the business page of your paper under Investment Funds. Those with bid and asked prices the same are closed-end funds. Those with a spread in price of bid and asked are open-end funds.

Mutual funds, better known because of enthusiastic salesmen, appeal to the small investor who sees them as a treasure island in the future. Indeed they can be if you investigate, choose carefully, and wait patiently.

Seemingly, anyone who can interest enough people to pay into a common fund until it totals $100,000, and can pass the requirements of the Securities and Exchange Commission can start a mutual fund. A number of bright young men are doing so. In addition, life insurance companies offer their own mutual funds. Hundreds of mutual funds exist and more pop up all the time.

TYPES AND TERMS TO UNDERSTAND

THE CLOSED-END TRUST OR FUND

Having a fixed number of shares, this type of fund is traded on the stock exchanges and over-the-counter. The price is regulated by supply and demand. If you want to buy or sell shares in a closed-end trust, you do so through your broker, paying a commission as on stocks.

THE OPEN-END OR MUTUAL FUND

Such a fund sells its own shares to the investor through trained salesmen, charges a handling fee and sales commission

What You Should Know About Trusts and Mutual Funds

of 6 to 9 percent. (Some mutual funds also sell shares through a broker.) The number of shares in a mutual fund is not limited, but constantly changing. The more buyers, the more shares. A mutual fund will redeem its shares at any time, usually without a fee. You can buy into it or get out of it at any time. Mutual funds advertise that their shares can be redeemed any day the stock market is open. The price of a share is based on net asset value (the total assets of the fund divided by the number of shares outstanding). The fund announces this share price in its financial statement. The difference between the bid and asked prices on the business page of the newspaper represents the sales commission.

LOAD FUND

The more you read about investment trusts and mutual funds, the more you will come across the term *load*. This refers to mutual funds and means the sales commission and other charges for shares sold. *Front-end load* means that when you sign a contract to buy a stated number of shares at regular investments, the sales commission and other expenses for opening the account are deducted from the first few payments, or from the first one if large enough. Also, a commission of 1 percent and a service charge of ½ percent are deducted from each regular investment. Investments may be as small as $10 a month, usually made over a period of years. Women who find it difficult to save on their own are attracted to this plan.

THE NO-LOAD FUND

Not usually sold by brokers or salesmen, you buy shares directly from the investment company. The way they make money on the deal is through a periodic management fee, usually ½ of 1 percent of the capital invested. The Investment Company Institute, 61 Broadway, New York, N.Y. 10006 lists about 60 no-load funds. If you write for it they will send you a list. You'll also find no-load shares listed in Arthur Wiesenberger's *Investment Companies,* published annually, on the shelves of most reference departments in libraries. The no-load fund, however, sells a minimum number of shares, sometimes $100 worth, sometimes $1,000.

Of course, when you buy into a fund, open- or closed-end, load or no load, you must expect to pay for the business end of the fund's keeping track of your shares. This fee, usually ½ of 1 percent is deducted from the annual income earned on your shares before payment of dividends.

The rest of this chapter will deal mainly with mutual or open-end funds.

FUNDS WOULD LIKE TO MANAGE YOUR MONEY

The spectacular rise of these funds from assets of half a million dollars 28 years ago to nearly 70 *billion* today is based on increased population and American affluence. More people have more money to invest. Naturally more and more funds would like to invest it for you.

Investors grab for shares, especially in some of the new "go-go" funds that have performed well the past year or two. In turn, offices of mutual funds found themselves snowed under with paper work, and in a similar situation to brokerage houses who saw the New York Stock Exchange cut down on trading days and time in an effort to straighten out the tangle. Some of the funds stopped selling their shares for a period of several months. Others would sell new shares only to shareholders already on the books.

To regulate new investment companies and protect early investors, Congress passed the Investment Act of 1940. Later, the Securities and Exchange Commission imposed other rules and regulations on the funds. Margin buying and short selling were ruled out, funds must register with the SEC, and certain rules govern management firms used by the funds. A mutual fund salesman must learn enough about a prospective shareholder to judge her financial ability to pay and to determine which one of the plans his fund offers is most suitable.

WHAT MAKES MUTUAL FUNDS POPULAR?

People invest in mutual funds because of many good features.

1. Security

You protect your capital and so offset the shrinking dollar. Statisticians report that in the past 100 years the United States economy has doubled every 16 or 17 years. Fixed income or fixed dollars are not enough to combat this inflation. If the fund you choose invests in American businesses that keep growing, if its shares, dividends, and capital gains distributions increase more than the economy, you protect your money no matter what happens to the dollar.

2. Convenience

After choosing your fund you have little to do except keep on investing. All you need do is mail in your checks. The fund's advisory firm will send you receipts, notices of next payment due (if you use a contractual plan), and convenient payment forms.

3. Diversification

Your fund may own as many as 100 different stocks in a dozen different types of industries. It is less risky to own shares in a fund than if you put all your money in one or two companies.

4. Management

For a fund to perform or be a success it needs good management. If it doesn't perform better than the stock market as a whole, management will lose as well as shareholders. Good management includes expert advice and analysis. No matter how small your investment, professionals will manage it for you.

5. Liquidity

Fund shares can be readily cashed. You can switch from one fund to another in the same mutual fund if your shares offer this privilege. If you have growth shares and want income shares, you can change, usually with a small record-keeping fee. (You must, though, pay capital gains tax.)

6. Systematic investment

You have automatic savings simply by instructing the fund to reinvest your dividends and capital gains distributions. Women on a small salary can, by regularly investing in mutual funds, accumulate capital. The contractual plan includes the hidden persuader of making you save regularly. You also take advantage of dollar-cost-averaging, whereby your regular payment buys more shares when the price is low than when it is high.

7. Systematic withdrawal

This appeals to more women perhaps than any other feature of mutual funds. You can count on a regular check from your investments. If you withdraw no more than 6 percent you are almost sure not to dig into your capital (barring a market crash).

8. Keogh plan

Through an act of congress in 1963, you may, if you are self-employed, set up your own retirement fund. You set aside 10 percent of your annual income up to $2,500. This money is deductible on your income tax, and any dividends or capital gains distributions or interest get deferred tax treatment while you're stashing it away. You must, though, put your retirement money in government-approved funds, such as U.S. retirement plan bonds, insurance, savings certificates, trust funds, or mutual funds.

If there are many good points about the funds, there are also limitations and faults which any interested woman must scrutinize.

1. Actual performance

To find out how well your fund has done you must add to the amount you have invested the dividends and capital gains distributions. Let's see why. First you have already reported these on your income tax return and paid tax on them. (The mutual fund figures this for you in a yearly statement.)

Suppose you paid a total of $10,000 for your mutual fund shares. Now after several years the shares are worth $14,000. This doesn't mean that you have a clear profit of $4,000. If you reinvested the capital gains and dividends, the total of these is counted as new investment money and must be added to the amount the shares cost.

Suppose the dividends and capital gains distributions on your shares amounted to $1,200. You could have withdrawn this amount periodically and spent it. Instead you chose to invest it in your fund (sensible, of course). Adding the $1,200 to your original investment of $10,000, your shares cost $11,200. Subtracting $11,200 from today's worth of your shares, $14,000, you have a gain of $2,800. If you held your shares six months or more you have a long-term capital gain. The dividends will count as income, of course, but the capital gains carry a tax of only half the amount.

2. Switching funds

When you switch from one fund to another in the same or a different mutual fund, the government will tap you on the shoulder for a capital gains tax. It makes no difference that you sell out of one fund and put your money right back into another. The law is that you have sold one batch of shares and bought another batch. If you have a capital gain you must pay tax on the sale. Here again dividends and capital gains distributions count as part of your cost and you pay income tax on half your gain.

3. High commissions

Critics complain that the front-end load earned by salesmen and management is far too high for services given. Criticism also points to the annual management fee of some funds which runs ½ of 1 percent a year of total assets. In the case of assets over $500 million the management fee is sometimes reduced on a sliding scale.

4. Contractual plan

This is a long-term contract for accumulating mutual fund shares. If you are the type that can't wait for the light to turn green and you quit early in the plan, you lose. Instead of being spread over the entire period of your investing, most of the sales commission for the full amount of the plan comes out of the first few payments. In defense of this front-end load or fee earned by salesmen and management, others argue that people pay the real estate salesman's commission before they take possession of a house. The car salesman gets his commission before you drive a car off the sales lot. Critics, though, shout that in the past high-pressure salesmen signed up customers for contractual plans when common sense made clear the customer couldn't keep up his contracted payments.

Of course you don't need to sign a contract. You can buy any number of shares any time you want. This is fine if you're a woman who will save on her own. The contract plan does make you save regularly.

5. Stability in a serious market depression

Experts say the mutual funds have never been tested in a steep market plunge. Mutual funds advertise they will redeem your shares whenever you want to sell. What would happen in a severe depression to the net asset value of a fund's shares if thousands of shareholders panicked and decided to sell at the same time? There would not necessarily be other buyers,

What You Should Know About Trusts and Mutual Funds

as in the case of closed-end shares where shares can't be sold without a buyer. Would the mutuals be able to cash in assets to cover such a run on shares without great loss?

Though mutual funds hold a big place in the investing program of countless persons, the limitations above propelled the funds into a storm of heavy criticism and an extensive investigation by the SEC. Criticism centers on these trouble spots:

1. High cost of the "load," the expenses and salesman's commission for signing you up.
2. High-pressure salesmanship.
3. Trap of the front-end load contractual plan, whereby initial costs, 6 to 9 ½ percent, come out of early payments instead of every payment made.
4. High management fee charged the funds by advisory firms.
5. That the average mutual fund's management has done no better than any informed investor (some have done far better, some not so well).
6. By overdiversification the funds fail to take advantage of big winners. In other words, their portfolios are spread too thin.

This leads us to another criticism of the funds, the part they play in market fluctuations. It may come as a surprise to some women that the institutions, which include not only mutual funds, but also pension funds, insurance companies, investment trusts and endowment trusts, banks and large estates, increasingly influence market activity in two ways.

● **Heavy buying**

Heavy buying by the institutions continues because Americans, in the middle of a boom period, keep pouring money into the funds. Institutions must compete for stocks with growth potential. What they'd like to discover is another IBM, Control Data or Xerox just aborning, and hold onto it until the stock triples or better. The competition pushes the price up. And as soon as individual investors notice a stock being heavily traded and bouncing upward, they too get into the act.

- **Heavy selling**

When you read in the business news page of the paper that a certain stock fell 21 points in one day on a large block of stock sold, in all probability some institution dumped its shares of that stock, taking the profits.

Take the way Control Data stock fell in August of 1968. Two big blocks of shares, 374,000 and 136,000 each, led the sell-off, which totaled 929,000 shares in one day. The stock dropped 16 ¾ points that day. The fourth quarter financial report of decreased earnings apparently triggered the sell-off. Though the names of sellers are not revealed on the NYSE, rumor had it that one or more mutual funds sold the biggest block of shares.

WHAT PRICE PERFORMANCE?

The performance of mutual funds depends on the shrewdness of their investments. If professional know-how tells them it's time to weed out stocks that are not growing, or that are vulnerable, the funds have an obligation to their shareholders to sell and buy more promising stocks. But you can see how the buying and selling of large blocks of shares can cause the market to spurt or plunge. Especially is this true of in-and-out trading. Critics have accused certain funds of buying heavily, pushing a stock price up, selling heavily, pushing the price down, and then rebuying at the low price. This, of course, is a speculative technique frowned on by the SEC. The fact remains, performance funds do buy and sell frequently in order to find winners.

It is not the concept of mutual funds that the SEC questions in a recent lengthy study. Instead the commission approves generally the fine record of mutual funds, but disapproves of unwise speculation with shareholders' money.

What You Should Know About Trusts and Mutual Funds

Let's now sit back and review. Should you lock up your money and wait a while before investing in mutual funds? On my desk lies a big $10 bill, the size issued in 1902, creased and crumbling with age. A curiosity piece, it is worth today in purchasing power, not $10 as printed front and back in 13 different ways, but much, much less. Figures that show the dollar of 1939 being worth 100 cents in spending power, recently listed it as being worth about 41 cents (October 1967).

What we women need is not to get involved with old-fashioned methods of keeping money safe, such as a piggy bank, or the one the old-timer recommended—"The best way to double your money is to fold it over twice and put it in your billfold." Nor should we be taken in by supersalesmen. We must be skeptical, serious-minded, aware of problems and difficulties in investing. Common sense tells us that neither fixed dollars nor fixed income is enough to combat inflation. A well-known authority says that if you have less than $5,000 to invest you should consider mutual funds, where the investigating is done for you and the stock is widely diversified. For women on limited incomes, investing in mutual funds may be the best possible way to protect and increase capital.

To Benefit Most from This Chapter:

1. Do you know anyone who owns mutual fund shares? If not, do a little sleuthing until you find at least two persons who will talk about their mutual funds.
2. Look in the stock quotations under Investment Funds for the bid and asked price of half a dozen funds.
3. Look up the prices of two closed-end funds. The bid and asked prices will be the same.
4. Send for the prospectus of two or three mutual funds.

Getting Your Money's Worth When You Buy Mutual Funds   11

You might think it easier to buy mutual funds than to choose your own portfolio of stocks, that it takes more work to buy individual stocks.

To put it bluntly, this may not be true. If you investigate several mutual funds and apply the following tests you will probably know enough about the market to investigate your own individual stocks. With the help of a good broker you can manage your own stocks, save part of the salesman's fee and other costs, and come up with just as good, if not better, results.

Still many women rely, with good reason, on the professional supervision mutual funds provide. For the woman with a modest amount to invest, mutual fund shares can be the answer.

Especially is this true for the young widow or divorcee, for those on small salaries who peer into the future and wonder what they will use for money. Being committed to small regular investments, if only $10 or $20 a month, can establish a habit that paves the way to accumulating or increasing capital. Owning mutual fund shares can give you confidence for investing in the stock market later when you have larger sums to invest.

Women with several thousand dollars to invest may also settle on mutual funds to advantage.

Getting Your Money's Worth When You Buy Mutual Funds

A woman I know (let's call her Ellen), near retirement, fell heir to $10,000. Her keen business sense directed her to invest the sum where it would grow. She chose shares in a sound mutual fund.

Ellen wanted to preserve her capital, but she planned to withdraw $75 a month. This was more than the 6 percent usually considered a safe amount to withdraw and still not reduce the principal. Based on the fund's past performance, she believed, and so did the salesman, that her shares would increase in value enough to offset the larger amount withdrawn.

The fund performed nicely in 1965 and 1966. Then an emergency caused Ellen to withdraw $600 worth of shares. She notified the mutual fund and promptly received the check, almost as easily as from a bank account.

The fund continued to perform well. After retirement Ellen decided she needed more income, so she asked to withdraw $100 a month, or almost 12 percent of her capital at the time. Four years after buying the shares, and after withdrawing a total of $4,600, Ellen's capital remains intact. Naturally, Ellen highly approves of that mutual fund in which she owns shares.

WHERE TO FIND OUT ABOUT FUNDS

How then does a woman go about selecting a mutual fund? Of course you can look in the phone book and choose a salesman, but you'll be more apt to get your money's worth if you do homework first. Think before you sign on the dotted line. Until you read and test and consider, you won't know which funds are geared to your needs. By talking to others, by checking the Investment Funds quotations in the paper, you probably already have half a dozen funds in mind.

An hour spent at the library in the business reference section or at the brokerage house can start you off. More than 500 investment trusts and mutual funds would like to sell you shares. Which one is for you?

Begin by pulling off the library shelves two huge books.

1. *Investment Companies,* annual volume put out by Arthur Wiesenberger Service Division of John Nuveen and Company. Read the opening pages to find out what the book is all about. Then look up the funds you are considering.
2. *Johnson's Investment Company Charts,* another big book, published annually. Study the performance charts and cellophane overlays. Compare the funds you want to know about with the average for all funds.
3. Another source of facts is *Forbes* magazine's annual issue on the funds, printed in August. Buy or inspect this at the library.
4. Still another source, *Barron's,* a weekly financial newspaper, prints once or twice a month a performance average of more than 300 leading funds. Figures show the average percentage change for the year so far and the average percentage change for the previous week.
5. *Reader's Guide to Periodical Literature* will steer you to informative magazine articles on the funds.

FACTS TO HELP YOU CHOOSE THE RIGHT FUND

The funds give any woman a choice, based on her needs. Most mutual funds offer shares in separate growth, income, balanced, or speculative funds.

Growth fund

A growth fund, invested in growth common stocks, pays small dividends. If you are checking a growth fund, compare the price of its shares with those of other mutual fund companies for a period of at least five years. Has the price gone up? You should plan to keep growth fund shares for several years at least, to take advantage of the fund's growth prospects.

Income fund

Invested in companies that pay regular high dividends, such funds show little growth in net asset value of shares. Though high income may be your object, you take the risk of your money remaining fixed or stable and not climbing with the economy.

Check the dividend rate, or yield, in relation to the share price. Did the fund pay dividends over a period of five years or more without lowering the price per share? If you had invested your money five years ago, what would it be worth today? Be sure to add up the dividends. Would you have prospered more if you had put your money in the bank? The income fund's chief merit derives from putting into it a set amount and drawing out regular amounts. It is especially attractive to women near retirement who see the payments as income, though they are not. They are partly interest and partly return of capital.

Balanced fund

Made up of common stocks, bonds, preferred stocks, U.S. Treasury notes, the balanced fund is really a fixed asset fund. If you look forward to a pension or annuity, insurance income, government savings bonds, and social security when you retire, you already have fixed income and should consider growth funds. A balanced fund, because it is conservative, is unlikely to perform as well as a growth fund, but the price of its shares will doubtless remain stable.

Speculative fund

You may consider a speculative fund because you want your investment to increase rapidly. You should understand, though, that sensational growth often spells added risk. Even if you do start in such a fund, later when you need income you will doubtless want to transfer your capital to a fund with high dividends. (Don't forget the capital gains tax.) Don't consider investing in a speculative fund unless you can take in stride the up and down price movements of its shares, and unless you can afford to leave your money invested for at least 10 years.

NET ASSET VALUE

Finally, check the net asset value (price per share) not just over the summer, but for the past 10 years. In a well-managed mutual fund the percentage rise should be faster than the market as a whole and the percentage decline slower. If the Dow Jones industrial average rises 10 percent in three months, how about the net asset value of the shares you are considering?

How did the price of your fund shares hold up in the market declines of 1966 and 1968? If you had invested money there a few years ago, would the fund have protected you against inflation?

But your choice should be based only partly on protection against inflation. You should also look for the promise of future growth and safety of capital.

Many funds, you will notice, have years of success behind them. Others are just getting off the ground. Let somebody else test these. Of late shareholders have called on some funds to redeem more shares a year than investors are buying. This means that the buyers are using the funds for short-term gains. In the eyes of fund management, shares are not intended for quick profits or short-term gains. Instead their shares are meant to be held. They should be bought with goals in mind, such as to start a business, education for the children, a trip to Europe, retirement.

THE IMPORTANCE OF FINDING THE RIGHT FUND

Some mutual funds have in the past, and doubtless will do

so in the future, paid off handsomely, but a woman needs to shop for the right one.

A performance survey made on 335 mutual funds showed the following results for the first eight months of 1968:[1]

>94 funds came up with gains of 10 percent
>19 funds increased 20 percent
>8 funds gained 30 percent
>62 of the funds lost money
>25 funds averaged a loss of 7 percent

You see, you might have gotten your money's worth, depending on which grouping you were in.

SEVEN WAYS TO TEST THE FUND YOU ARE INTERESTED IN

1. Size

Bigness alone—number of outstanding shares and total assets—does not necessarily win a blue ribbon. The more assets a fund has, though, the more cash its managers get, since they are paid on a percentage basis of total assets. That's what a fund is in business for—to make money. That you make money is a side issue.

2. Management

If you invest in a fund because you are too busy or lack self-confidence to run down your own stocks, be sure the fund you choose is well-managed and that you get expert counsel. As pointed out before, management is one of the items you pay for when you buy mutual funds. If you don't get top management, the fund is not a bargain.

3. Performance

How have the fund's shares done compared to the market as a whole or the Dow Jones industrial average or other indexes?

[1]Carlton Smith and Richard Putnam, "Mutual Funds Winners Again." St. Paul, Minnesota: St. Paul Pioneer Press, Sept. 16, 1968,©NEA Special Services.

In assessing a fund's performance, compare the way the funds as a whole advanced in the same period. If *Johnson's Investment Company Charts* average shows a 12 percent increase for all funds and your fund shows only an 8 percent increase in the value of its shares, you're not getting your money's worth. If several funds show increases while your fund comes up with a decrease, take another look before you buy.

4. Cost

Is the sales charge in line with other mutual funds? See *Forbes* annual report on the funds for a comparison of sales charges.

5. Yield

Yield means the return on your investment, the dividends you receive, calculated as a percentage of the price per share. To figure the yield on a fund that interests you, divide the dividends per share for the year by the current asked price. A fund paying 13 cents a share, with the price of the share $8.80, would yield 1.4 percent. Next figure the percent of increase or decrease paid on a share compared to a year ago. Compute dividends only. Capital gains distributions represent a return of capital.

If the price of your shares climbs consistently, perhaps you can close your eyes to a reduced dividend.

Wiesenberger states that at the beginning of 1969 yields on mutual funds ranged from less than 1 percent to about 5 percent.

This, of course, is not as much as some savings accounts produce.

6. Annual report and prospectus

Mailed to prospective customers, as well as all investors in the fund, these give you clues about the fund's performance. Read the fine print. Check the common stocks in which your fund invests. Keen competition among the funds causes some to try to outperform others by heavy in-and-out trading and buying speculative stocks.

A fund heavily invested in speculative stocks or a fund which specializes in in-and-out trading to chalk up performance in the short term (six months or less) is looking for instant growth. *Result:* The fund is more speculative than others that invest in sound growth stocks and wait for natural upward growth.

7. Broker

Because he will not receive the high sales commission mutual fund salesmen receive, your broker's viewpoint of the fund you are considering may not agree with the salesman's. Test this by getting his opinion.

You may also want to consider *no-load* funds. Usually two or three top performers each year are no-load funds.

Fairly new on the investment scene are *dual funds*—closed-end funds with a definite lifetime. Instead of all shares in a dual fund getting dividends and capital gains distributions, the dual fund offers two kinds of shares: (1) income shares, on which the fund pays dividends, and (2) capital shares, on which the fund distributes capital gains. (Capital gains, you recall, come about when the company sells some of its common stock holdings at a gain.)

FUNDS UNDER FEDERAL INVESTIGATION

Since late 1966 the Securities and Exchange Commission has pried into some of the practices of the funds. In 1968 the SEC frowned on many funds for heavy trading in the more speculative stocks of the American Stock Exchange and unlisted or over-the-counter stocks.

Such practices are contrary to the previous sales pitch of

most mutual funds. Originally aimed at the small investor, the mutual funds advertised a platform that included:

1. Protection of capital
2. Diversification
3. Long-term investment
4. Liquidity

If a fund trades big blocks of shares on a short-term basis, it will end up with large capital gains. Quarterly or once a year these capital gains must be distributed to shareholders, by check or additional shares. Either way, you pay capital gains income tax. Of course there's nothing wrong with capital gains—quite the opposite. But when the chief way your fund earns capital gains is by short-term trading in speculative stocks, you are not getting your money's worth.

Frequent in-and-out trading by your fund to increase assets or to show performance may also add up to less dividends than in previous years. If at the same time the net asset value of the fund's shares shows little increase, the woman investor needs to take another look before buying.

POINTS TO CHECK BEFORE YOU BUY

Does the fund you are investigating allow you to change from one fund to another (within the company) without an additional sales charge?

Does the fund allow you to reinvest your dividends and capital gains distributions without a charge? Though this may not be a detriment when you add everything up, you should be sure.

Has the fund come up with an outstanding performance in the past five years at least? Don't be taken in by a flash in the pan. One new fund, admittedly based on in-and-out trading, uses computers to monitor over 2,000 stocks in order to make quick trades. The fund is not interested in investing as such, it says, but in making money.

Caution: Even outstanding performance over the past five

years does not guarantee similar performance over the next five. But it gives you a basis for forming your opinion.

It wouldn't hurt for you to compare the performance of the common stock of several sound growth companies over the same period of time.

Shopping for the right mutual fund, like any other major purchase, is only a bargain if you get your money's worth. First comes your decision for the fund itself. Then you choose the sub-fund or division your fund offers that is most attractive to you. Certainly you can feel comfortable about the safety of money you invest in funds you have carefully investigated. A fund that has operated and proved itself for a number of years is as safe as any sound stock investment in individual companies. All investment and mutual funds must register with the Securities and Exchange Commission. They must reveal to the public, or their shareholders, in quarterly and annual reports and prospectuses, their assets and liabilities, income and profits, stocks they invest in, amount of annual management fees, and they must abide by other SEC rules.

Because of these facts, a young businessman friend of mine sold all his stock holdings and put them into mutual funds. Previously he had done rather well in the stock market. I wondered why the switch.

"I know that I can manage my own money," he said, "but it does take time. For the years while my boys are small I'll let the funds manage for me. That way I'll have more evenings to spend with my family."

After your first stint of investigation, mutual funds take the work out of investing. Instead of working from scratch each time you buy more shares, everything is packaged for you. You also reap the benefits of professional management and supervision on your investment no matter how small it is. Besides, you achieve a degree of diversification not possible in a like investment in common stocks. All this doesn't mean, however, that you should put your certificate in the safety box and never check up on your mutual fund.

QUESTIONS TO PONDER IF YOU WANT TO GET YOUR MONEY'S WORTH

1. Will mutual funds take charge of your money and do a better job of managing it and protecting it than you are likely to do? Is the management investing as you would? That is, buying common stocks of good quality in sound growth companies?
2. If you have already taken charge of your money, are you satisfied with your own management?
3. What about the cost and commission on buying mutual fund shares? This is usually about 8½ percent of the amount invested. The cheapest management you can get, of course, is yourself.
4. What does your fund pay in dividends, either by check or in additional shares?
5. What funds of the hundreds available will best meet your needs and objectives?

Finally, ponder these words of wisdom, not original with me: A woman can only get her money's worth in any investment if:

- She protects her capital against inflation,
- She receives a steady income on her capital, and
- Over the long run she sees both her capital and income increase.

Anything less is not a bargain.

To Benefit Most from This Chapter:

1. Decide on at least three funds to investigate further.
2. Spend an hour in the library with *Johnson's Investment Company Charts* and *Arthur Wiesenberger's Investment Companies*.
3. Check your funds in *Forbes* annual survey on investment and mutual funds.

If you do your homework you should have the confidence to take positive action. Don't delay; buy your first mutual fund shares now.

Keeping Essential Records   12

Some investors take care of their own stock certificates by keeping them in a safety deposit box at the bank. Stock certificates are much too valuable to leave lying around at home in a desk drawer. Other investors never see their stock certificates, preferring to leave them with the brokerage firm in "street" name for safe-keeping.

Either way you'll need to keep records. Even if record-keeping is not your favorite occupation, once you understand its importance, you will discipline yourself to be businesslike.

Naturally, with only one or two stocks to watch, your bookkeeping won't take too much time. But looking ahead to the future when you may own shares in 10 or 15 companies, what you learn today about keeping essential records will pay off.

CERTIFICATES IN STREET NAME

If you decide to leave your certificates with your brokerage house, their office will do a lot of book work for you. They will:

1. Keep your certificates in their vault. (Certificates in their name, designated as yours.)
2. Charge any new stock you buy to your account until your check arrives.

3. Advise you of any rights, conversions of stocks, or tender offers concerning any of your companies.
4. Exercise your rights according to your instructions.
5. Send you recent stock analyses of your companies, especially when some change is imminent.
6. Mail you a statement once a month of any dividends due you, or if you so instruct, credit the dividends to your account.
7. Mail you a monthly statement of the condition of your account.
8. Mail you a year-end statement of dividends reported to the Internal Revenue Service, and all transactions in your account for the year.
9. Quickly and conveniently sell stock for you. All you need do is pick up the phone. If you take charge of your certificates, you would have to make a trip to your safety deposit box at the bank, then present the certificate to your broker and sign it. The brokerage house takes care of all this if your certificate is in street name.
10. Provide credit for you should you decide to buy on margin or short sale. When 80 percent margin is in effect the brokerage firm will lend you 20 percent of the value of the stock you want to buy (See Chapter 4, Picking Up the Jargon). The firm does this on the strength of your certificates they hold in their own, or street name.

The brokerage firm makes no charge for its services to you, but if you have a margin account it assumes the right to lend your certificates to others for short sales and margin buying. The certificates are not actually in your name, but in the brokerage firm's name.

ADVANTAGES OF PLACING CERTIFICATES IN STREET NAME

Holding certificates in street name would be a necessity

for a trader where timing is all-important. But many investors, too, prefer the convenience of this arrangement. Advantages include:

1. Borrowing power, which makes it easy to zero in on favorable market conditions.
2. Easier to reinvest dividends, which is a spur to regular saving.
3. Less record-keeping for the stockholder.

Moreover, what nearly happened to a woman I know can't happen to anyone who keeps her certificates in street name.

Anita Barnes, we'll call her, had help opening her mail—three preschool children. Because of the pile of junk mail, the children had a good time playing postman while Mamma opened the regular mail. Quickly Anita separated the day's delivery into two piles—letters and bills in one, junk mail in the other. The latter she handed to the children. Gummed labels in one envelope kept them happy playing postman while Anita read her letters.

Not until sometime later, when she told the children to pick up the scattered envelopes and papers, did she snatch one stiff page from the floor. She held in her hand a stock certificate for shares of stock issued in a stock split. Her children had decorated the certificate with the gummed labels.

Yes, of course, carelessness entered in, but the certificate had arrived in the same sized manila envelope as an ad for magazine subscriptions with its gummed labels. Anita had mistaken the envelope with the certificate for a piece of junk mail.

DISADVANTAGES OF LEAVING CERTIFICATES IN STREET NAME

Critics of the street system complain that in recent years brokerage offices have had more book work than they can cope with properly. This resulted often in slow reports to customers and certificate "fails" to transfer agents (failure of the selling brokerage firm to deliver the actual stock certificates sold).

In their own defense brokerage firms cite unprecedented trading volume. Several times in 1968, 20-million share volume days topped the long-time record of more than 16 million shares traded one day back in 1929.

Not only investors who leave their certificates in street name, though, experience delays and inconvenience due to heavy volume. So do investors who prefer to keep track of their own certificates. I am one of these. Though I have had excellent advice and help from my broker, I have waited six weeks to two months to receive a balance due me for a stock transaction, and without interest! Also for more than two years I have struggled to get my name correctly spelled on the stencil of the brokerage office. I know that an "e" or an "a" makes little difference in the spelling of my name. But computers don't. As a result I have two account numbers with several companies. I get two dividend checks. Once I lost out on exercising rights on a share of stock. With two accounts at the company's transfer agent, I received two notices of rights. Because I was new at the game I returned both cards stating I would exercise my rights. In time I received the new shares and a small check on each account for a fractional share. The two fractional share credits combined would have allowed me to get one more share.

Unprecedented volume and antiquated bookkeeping systems in many back offices of brokerage firms impelled the exchanges to close an hour earlier in 1968 and then all day Wednesdays for most of the year, in the hope of cutting down volume and catching up with paper work.

Many brokerage houses have already converted to computers, and others are doing so as rapidly as possible. Much of the blame lies with the time-honored stock certificate, which takes personal handling. However, death of the certificate may be in the offing. Instead of a certificate, we may one day receive an IBM card record of all stock transactions.

Despite all this, many investors prefer leaving their certificates in street name. If you do, don't conclude that all record-keeping is out of your hands. Brokerage firms do occasionally make errors. More important, you need to keep records for income tax returns.

BE PROFESSIONAL BY KEEPING THESE MINIMUM RECORDS

If you leave your certificates in the street name, the minimum records you will want to keep are:

1. In a notebook in a safe place list the date you bought or sold shares, the name of the stock, number of shares, price per share, commission, tax, total amount. You need this record to figure your cost base for income tax purposes should you sell the stock in the future.

For example, suppose you bought:

1960	Stock L	50 shares @ $35	$1,750
1964	Stock L	50 shares @ 41	2,050
1967	Stock L	50 shares @ 43	2,150

Suppose also that the stock goes up in 1969 to $45 a share, and you decide to sell 50 shares. The shares you bought in 1960 are worth $2,250, a gain of $500. Those you bought in 1964 are also worth $2,250, but with a gain of only $200. And the ones you bought in 1967 show a gain of only $100. The amount of your capital gain that you report on your income tax depends on which batch of shares you sell at this time. Perhaps you would rather claim a capital gain on the most recent shares you bought. Unless you can positively identify your shares, your cost base will be that of the earliest date of purchase.

So then you must specify to your broker in writing just which shares you want to sell, identified by date of purchase and cost. In turn he should send you a written confirmation of the specification within a reasonable time. If you can identify your stock in this manner, the government, for tax purposes, assumes that the stock you specified you wanted sold is the stock sold, even though a very different lot or certificate is delivered to the transfer agent by your brokerage firm.

2. Save all confirmation slips from your broker as well as the monthly statement. Verify these as soon as you receive them.

3. For your own satisfaction keep a monthly comparison sheet. (Figure 1) This will tell you at a glance how your stock investments stand.

Figure 1

Date Bot	Name of Company	No. of Shares	Total Cost	Current Value and Share Price					
				Jan. 26	Feb. 24	Mar. 27	Apr. 28	May 27	June 30
11/1/66	Stock A	100	@ 40 $4,000	38 3800	37 3700	38 3800	39 3900	39 3900	40 4000
3/4/67	Stock B	50	@ 31 1,550	36 1800	37 1850	39 1950	37 1850	36 1800	37 1850
2/15/68	Stock C	10	@ 77 770	79 790	81 810	85 850	85 850	86 860	87 870
	Totals		$6,320	6390	6360	6600	6600	6560	6720

You might also add the Dow Jones Industrial Average and Standard and Poor's composite average.

Under the monthly heading the small number is the price per share to the nearest whole number. If the price of Stock A is quoted as 38-3/8 I record the price as 38. The larger figure is the value of the number of shares I hold on the day I take inventory.

You may also figure what percent your holdings have increased or decreased over the previous month.

4. Any expenses such as a stock magazine subscription, or rental of a safety deposit box.

5. Finally you should keep a record of your annual net worth. This should include all your capital, insurance, bank accounts, real estate, and government bonds, as well as

common stock. But for our purposes here we'll consider stocks only.

CERTIFICATES IN YOUR OWN NAME

If you decide to keep track of your own certificates, you should keep them in a safe place. If you leave them lying around at home in a dresser drawer they might be lost, stolen, or destroyed by fire. Of course you could write the transfer agent for a duplicate. But obtaining a new stock certificate is a lengthy and costly process, and you would probably have to post a surety bond to protect the corporation and the transfer agent.

WHAT YOU NEED TO KEEP YOUR OWN RECORDS

1. SAFETY DEPOSIT BOX

The best protection is to rent a small safety box at your bank. The cost, less than $10 a year, is tax deductible.

2. A NOTEBOOK

Have a separate page for each stock you own. In it write:

Name of company and address.
Type of industry.
Name of transfer agent and address.
Certificate number.
Date bought, number of shares, price per share, total cost, including commission and state tax if any.
Cost base per share (See Chapter 14, What to Do About Your Income Tax).
Date and amount of dividends paid.
Date sold, certificate number, number of shares sold, price per share, total, commission and tax.
Capital gain or loss.

You can make up your own forms for keeping records on each stock, or, to make your bookkeeping easier, buy printed

Keeping Essential Records

forms. I like the printed forms and three-ring binder I found in the local stationery store, illustrated in Figure 2. The form has room for all the information needed for careful record-keeping on individual stocks.

3. CONFIRMATION SLIPS

The brokerage firm will send you a confirmation within five days of your buy or sell order. Verify all figures and file it in the safety box with your stock certificate. When you sell the stock attach the confirmation slip to the buy confirmation slip and file with your income tax papers in a safe place.

4. MANILA FILE FOLDERS

One for each company you own stock in. Collect news items, annual reports and letters from the company, and any pertinent articles relating to your stock.

5. RECORD OF EXPENSES

Include all expenses for your investments, such as safety box rental, anything you paid for investment advice, financial magazine subscription, books on investing.

6. MONTHLY COMPARISON SHEET (See Figure 1)

7. GRAPH OF EACH STOCK

A graph is a picture of the rise and fall of your stock, and as such may help you see what your shares are doing. The simplest graph shows monthly dates across the top, one sheet for each stock. Up the left side you write in figures representing the price of the stock. You might show on the right-hand side figures representing the Dow Jones industrial average or some other average. At the end of the year you can see at a glance how your stock behaved compared to the averages. Graph sheets can be bought at any stationery store.

8. ANNUAL COMPARISON OF ASSETS

Again this should include all your capital—real estate,

Figure 2 [1]

[1] Used by permission. Pfenig & Snyder, Mi-Reference, Columbus, Ohio 43212.

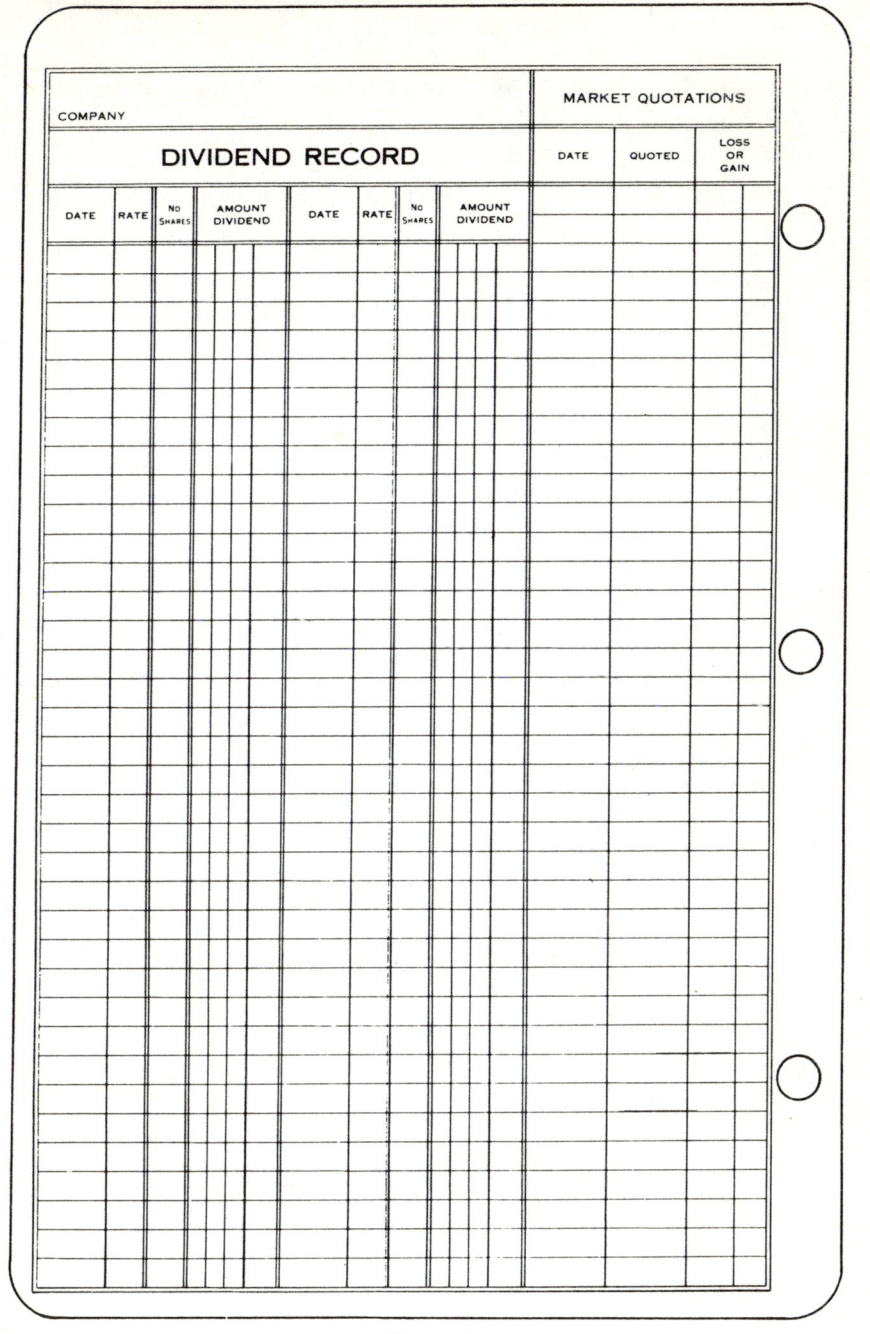

Figure 2

insurance, bank accounts, cash, government bonds, as well as common stock.

For annual comparison of increase or decrease in your stock portfolio, you set down the market value of all your stocks at the first of the year. Then put down any new capital added during the year, including dividends reinvested. Deduct the amount of any stock sold, less capital gains tax you will have to pay. Figure the total value of your stocks from quotations on the last business day of the year. Figure the difference between these two amounts—value at the beginning of the year, plus additions, less sales and the value at the end of the year. How have you done? What is your percentage increase or decrease?

You should review all your stock holdings at least once a year, and oftener if some unusual circumstance comes up, such as a plunge in market price or a drop in earnings. A mistake some women investors make is to become so attached to a certain stock they think they must hang onto it until they die. Nothing could be deadlier for your success as your own investment manager.

At least once a year review your stocks and compare the previous year's records of:

Increase in sales
Increase in earnings
Increase in profit margin
Increase in dividends
Price-earnings ratio (See Chapter 6, How to Read a Financial Report.)

Ask yourself: Is this still the high-grade stock I thought it was when I bought it? If not, it is better to get rid of it at once and invest in a good stock than to run the risk of losing even more.

9. INCOME TAX RECORDS

Various authorities cite three and one-half years as the limit for keeping tax records. But if a taxpayer makes an error the Internal Revenue Service can go back six years. If intent to defraud is suspected, IRS agents can go back indefinitely.

Until that happy day when household computers or microfilm become as commonplace as electric can openers, you simply *must* keep accurate records. The best way is to begin in a small way when you own only one or two stocks.

To Benefit Most from This Chapter:

Set up a record page for each stock you own, using the suggestions in this chapter.

The Art of Giving 13

You may feel you have scarcely enough money to see you through sunny days, let alone rainy weather. Giving any substantial amount of money never enters your mind. Still, anything you learn now about the art of giving may mean money in your billfold in the future. When the time comes that your capital does increase, you'll want to do more with it than just count your stock certificates filed away in a safety deposit box at the bank. After all, the way a woman *spends* her money indicates her sense of values.

A woman on her own or one who, through divorce or death of her husband, manages the family income must make decisions about how to spend money. This means deciding how much to spend for current needs, how much to save for the future, how much to give to the church, how much for helping others more needy.

A young woman with her first job probably won't lose any sleep over whether or not to give any of her money to help build a new wing for the local hospital. Nor will the young widow faced with educating three children consider giving $10,000 right now to her college. But many others will do so now or in the future when they do have capital to share. And the future, the sage has said, usually arrives before we expect it.

Some women even experience the staggering knowledge that their capital is appreciating (or increasing) faster than

The Art of Giving

they can spend it. This happened to Milton Hershey, of chocolate fame, and his wife.

Understanding the basic meaning of philanthropy—love for mankind—the Hersheys felt a responsibility to those in need. His wife suggested they found a school for unfortunate boys. Today the school supports itself, housing 1,500 boys from kindergarten through high school. The boys and counselors live in cottages and on farms on 10,000 acres surrounding Hershey, Pennsylvania.

As the Hersheys poured money into the school project and turned over shares of Hershey stock to it, their gifts snowballed. The school prospered. Through Hershey Estates and other trust funds, the school owns stock in 38 businesses, and gave money for a medical center in Hershey, operated by Pennsylvania State University.

From early days private philanthropy built American churches, colleges, libraries, parks, and organized foundations. Andrew Carnegie, Henry Ford, Andrew Mellon, John D. Rockefeller, and many others gave millions in benevolences. We read about such gifts on the front page of the newspaper. But equally important, countless middle-class persons in every bracket of income share their wealth with the world's needy. Added to these we find many women who would like to give money to their children, their grandchildren, colleges, and churches.

As women we probably sense more than men do the serious financial need of many of our nation's schools, churches, and humane institutions. That's why we need to cultivate an attitude of stewardship of what we possess, and face our responsibility to support such organizations. Along with the happiness that comes to those who share their wealth, women can expect tax savings if they plan ahead. Our tax laws are generally favorable to those who give to charity. The art of giving requires, besides a heart of love, clearheaded planning in order to take full advantage of such tax savings.

THE IMPORTANCE OF UNDERSTANDING FACTS ABOUT GIFTS

1. Gift tax

Many women have never heard of the gift tax. If you give away more than $3,000 in money, securities, or other property in any one year to any one person, you must report this to the Government and pay a gift tax. You make a special gift tax return.

Even paying the gift tax works somewhat to your advantage, for that tax is only 75 percent of what the federal estate tax would be if the amount of the gift remained in your estate at your death. Depending on your set-up, a gift can save up to 100 percent of the estate tax that might otherwise be payable.

2. Annual exclusion

You may give up to $3,000 in cash, securities, real estate, or any other property to one or any number of individuals each year without paying the gift tax. (A husband and wife may give up to $6,000 together.) For example you might give $3,000 to your son, $3,000 to your daughter-in-law, and $3,000 to each of three grandchildren in a single year (if your capital permits such largess) and still not have to pay a gift tax.

For an older woman with holdings that yield more income than she needs, so that her capital appreciates regularly, such annual gifts can reduce her estate and consequently reduce federal estate taxes at her death, leaving more for her children and favorite charities. Added attraction for any woman is realizing that such gifts made during her lifetime can lift a heavy burden of debt or of educating her grandchildren from a son's or daughter's shoulders right now. Such gifts will be of far more value now than if received after her death when the son or daughter may be prospering on his own.

The Art of Giving

3. Lifetime exemption

A woman may give in her lifetime a total of $30,000 to individuals, all at once or over a period of years. But any gifts in excess of the lifetime exemption (and above the $3,000 annual exclusion) will be taxed. A husband and wife may give jointly double the lifetime exemption or $60,000.

The gift tax does not apply to gifts to the church or charitable institutions.

4. Uniform Gifts to Minors Act

Most states administer this or a similar statute, which permits gifts of money as well as securities to minor children. Many parents with adequate income for emergencies and enough to see them to life's exit make gifts of stocks to their young children. You need to consider two points here:

1. Are you willing to give up control of such property? You must give it with no strings attached.
2. Will your child misuse such gifts and spend the money recklessly? (You run into tax problems if you name yourself as custodian. In such instances the government considers the money a part of your estate. It is better to name some other custodian.)

Grandparents, on the other hand, may make such gifts, naming the child's parent as custodian. The property passes out of the hands of the grandparent and can be administered by the custodian parent for the child's benefit.

The following could easily happen. Mrs. Boardman set up special bank accounts for each of her four grandchildren, naming their mother as custodian. Each year Mrs. Boardman adds to the account (less than $3,000 for each child so she pays no gift tax). Interest accrues. When a grandchild reaches age 21 the money is his. Or the parent may have used it for the child's education. Mrs. Boardman has no control over the bank accounts, so the money is out of her estate for federal tax purposes—unless she dies within three years of making the gifts (see page 205).

As long as the interest per year, added to any other income the child makes, amounts to less than $900 nobody pays income tax on such bank accounts. Even if the child's income and the interest should amount to more than $900 a year in his teens, his tax rate would doubtless be less than the grandmother's. When the child withdraws the money from the bank account to pay for college tuition or some other purpose, it is not taxed again, since it was income during the years the bank account grew.

When you give *appreciated* stocks, your cost base (what you paid for the stock) is the new owner's cost base. See Chapter 14, What To Do About Your Income Tax. For *depreciated* stocks the cost base is the fair market value at time of gift. Should you give stocks valued above the $30,000 lifetime exemption or $3,000 annual exclusion and so have to pay a gift tax, the amount of the gift tax is added to your cost base.

WAYS TO MAKE CONTRIBUTIONS THAT WILL BENEFIT YOU

Many conscientious women add to the amount of their tax simply because they don't understand favorable tax treatment for contributions. We know that federal laws allow deductions (and so a reduction in the amount of tax paid) on income tax returns for gifts to religious, educational, and other charitable organizations. What may not be so well-known is that we can further reduce the amount of income tax by various methods of giving. I had to have some of these explained to me.

Whatever amount we women cut from our total income by shrewd methods of giving means less income tax to pay and added capital. Instead of taking the standard 10 percent for all deductions, it may pay you to itemize them.[1]

1. Deduction for gifts up to 30 percent of income

At present we may deduct up to 30 percent of our adjusted gross income for gifts to qualified organizations in

[1] Proposed change in the Tax Reform Bill before Congress at this writing would increase the standard deduction to 15 percent, to a maximum of $2,000.

any one year. Adjusted gross income means total income less allowable expenses in gaining that income, and any other allowable items. The Internal Revenue Service prints a list of qualified organizations, chiefly cultural, religious, educational, and non-profit, such as the Salvation Army, United Fund, Boy Scouts.

Should you donate more than 30 percent of your income in a year, federal tax laws allow you to spread the larger gift over five years of tax returns, or until the amount of the gift deduction is used up.

To illustrate, Mrs. Truman wants to donate $2,000, in memory of her husband, toward a new dormitory for the college he attended. Her adjusted gross income is $7,000 for the year. Throughout the year she also gave a total of $700 to her church, United Fund, and various small charities, a total of $2,700 for the year. Thirty percent of her adjusted gross income comes to $2,100, leaving a difference of $600. She may carry over this difference to the next year, or up to five years, as a deduction.

2. Gifts of appreciated stocks

Mrs. Truman might have saved even more by giving the college a long-term capital gain asset of $2,000 worth of appreciated shares of stock (stock that has increased in value over her cost). The value of the gift would be the market value of the shares on the day they changed hands. Her income tax deduction would be the full $2,000 (spread over more than one year as above). But even though the shares had appreciated since she bought them, she would not report a capital gain nor pay tax on it. In case of benevolent gifts, the government does not consider a long-term (six months) capital gain as taxable.

Suppose Mrs. Truman bought the shares for $900, held them for four years, when the market value reached $2,000—a capital gain of $1,100. If she sold the shares and gave the amount to the college, she would realize a capital gain of $1,100, a long-term gain because she had held them longer than six months. She would then pay income tax on 50 percent of the capital gain or on $550. By giving the shares outright to the college, she would not pay a tax on her capital gain. She would also take a charitable deduction on her return for the gift.

If Mrs. Truman favors this stock and wants it in her portfolio, she may buy new shares of the stock at once. This works to her advantage since she now has a new, higher cost base to use when she wants to sell the shares in the future.

3. Depreciated stocks

In giving stock that has depreciated in value, the opposite approach yields the best tax advantage. Instead of donating shares of stock, you sell the stock, give the proceeds to your church or other charity, and report the capital loss on your income tax return. Of course, you take a charitable deduction for the sum you give to the church.

4. Bargain sale

Bargain sale is a legitimate method whereby you *sell* your appreciated shares to the charitable organization at your cost price. By so doing you avoid a capital gains tax. You take a charitable deduction for the difference between your cost and the present market value, and you get the amount you paid for the shares to reinvest.

For example, you own 80 shares of Company S stock, with a cost base of $57 a share, or $4,560 (broker's commission not taken into account). At the present market value of a share, $69, the shares are worth $5,520. You sell the shares to the Union Gospel Mission at your cost, $4,560. This represents a bargain to the Mission, since they can at once sell the shares for the present market value, $5,520. You take a charitable deduction for your gift of $960, and do not pay a capital gains tax.

You may, if you choose, buy new Company S stock with the $4,560 the Mission paid you for the bargain shares. Since the shares cost more today than your old shares, your cost base on the new stock will be higher. When you do sell the Company S shares, your capital gain, on which you will have to pay income tax, may not be as great as if you had retained the first shares.

5. Gift annuity

Here you pay shares of stock to a qualified organization in return for a fixed annual income, determined by your age and life expectancy. As long as you live you will receive a regular payment, but when you die the property goes to the church or organization. You take a charitable deduction on your tax return in the year you make the gift. Of course, if the gift is more than 30 percent of your annual income, the amount can be prorated for five years or until used up.

But you do not take a deduction for the full amount of the shares turned over to your church or school. Here's why. The government has worked out life expectancy tax tables that show the amount you can deduct. When you contract with a qualified organization to receive regular payments in exchange for your stock, the amount you can deduct depends on your life expectancy. You pay income tax on the part of the annuity payment that represents interest.

Such annuities cannot, however, compete with commercial annuities. Still you have the satisfaction of making a generous gift while still living. Here, too, if you give appreciated stocks or property, you will probably eliminate the capital gains tax. This plan, though, is irrevocable. You cannot change your mind. Once you give the shares they are out of your estate forever.

6. Life income plan

In this plan, you give your shares to a college or other favorite charity, reserving the right to the dividends paid. Sometimes you may also direct that the dividends, upon your death, go to your child or another person. Accountants figure your charitable deduction by computing your life expectancy. This plan, too, cannot be revoked.

7. Short-term charitable trust

Here you transfer an income-producing property or security to a church or charity for not less than two years.[2] The organization holds the securities in trust, receives the income from them. At the end of the agreed time, the property reverts to the owner. During the short-term trust the income from the property is not reported as income by the owner, nor is it considered as a charitable deduction. This sometimes works well for the woman in a high-income bracket, or one who is self-employed and receives high income for several years.

8. Revocable charitable trust

A woman hands over securities to a trustee, directing that the dividends be paid to a charitable organization. This trust can be revoked or recalled, but if the trust is in effect at the woman's death, the stocks revert to the organization. Such a trust is counted as part of her estate for federal taxes, and the estate can claim an offsetting charitable deduction.

9. Outright gift of stocks

Many women, as they grow older, think more about gifts to charity and the church. For one who wants to leave a gift of $5,000 or $10,000 or more to her church or charity, experts advise giving the amount now instead of by will. At the same time, the woman should reserve lifetime rights to income from the stocks.

The federal government allows a partial deduction for such gifts, not a full deduction as in the case of giving the stock with no strings attached. The allowable deduction is figured on your life expectancy.

---

[2] Proposed change in the Tax Reform Bill before Congress at this writing would increase the term to ten years.

The Art of Giving

Most charitable institutions stand to gain in any of the above arrangements, even though you outlive your expected years. Since securities have in the past appreciated greatly, what was once a small gift can in a period of 20 years or so increase to a handsome amount. Besides the gift will outlive you.

If you plan to make any large gift, check with your attorney as well as the one you want to give to for advice on how to make the best use of existing tax laws.

10. Matching gifts

Certain corporations conduct a "Matching Gifts Program," whereby they will match, or sometimes double, any gift an employee makes to an eligible school of higher education. Check with personnel management of the company for which you work.

11. Round-about gift

Even as I prepared the pages of this book, I discovered another method of giving. An accountant, formerly an IRS employee, checked several chapters for accuracy. When I asked for his fee he replied, "Just make a check payable to Bethel College, St. Paul, Minnesota. That's my way of making a gift to the school." The accountant can take a charitable deduction for the amount of the gift to the college. Such assigned income must be reported as income in order to be claimed as a charitable deduction.

No matter what form your giving takes, it must be legally transferred, not remain in your control, in order to qualify for tax reduction.

One recent study shows that women value money for what it can do for others as well as themselves. When women think of capital as a means of security, independence, and helping the world's needy, they tend to forget about acquiring a lot of immediate, material things.

Credit goes to Booker T. Washington who, a long time ago, wrote these words on the art of giving. "The longer I live the more I am convinced that the one thing worth living for... is the privilege of making someone more happy and more useful."

To Benefit Most from This Chapter:

Most of the methods given in this chapter will probably have more meaning for you in the future than right now. Tuck them away in your subconscious labeled *stewardship*.

What to Do About Your Income Tax 14

To fail to declare any part of your income is a serious offense against the government, but to fail to deduct any amount you are rightfully entitled to deduct is a waste of money and an offense against your management of capital entrusted to you.

REPORT YOUR INCOME ACCURATELY

Certain income, of course, need not be reported—social security payments, disability payments, insurance payments that represent return of capital, non-taxable dividends on certain securities, gifts. Interest on insurance, though, is taxable, except for a widow's $1,000 exemption. All other income should be reported.

True, the law does not require corporations to report dividends of less than $10 a year paid to any one stockholder. Now that most corporations use computers the likely conclusion is that they will report all dividends. It would entail too much expense to exclude small dividends from reports.

If for no other reason than to avoid a kickback, you should scrupulously report all taxable income. More than a joke lies behind the story of the Internal Revenue Service agent who called in a woman taxpayer and said, "Your return just blew three tubes in the computer."

PROPER WAYS TO REDUCE YOUR INCOME TAX

While every dollar added to your income means more tax to pay, there are proper ways to reduce the income on which you pay tax. An increase of $100 in your income means, if your income should put you in the 20 percent bracket, that you then have only $80 to spend after taxes. In other words, to keep $100 you must earn $125.

But reducing your year's income $100 by legitimate deductions is a net savings of $120—$100 plus $20 tax.

Before considering how you can take advantage of tax deductions, perhaps an explanation of some terms will help.

Capital gains is any gain over your original cost that you make in the sale of a piece of property such as shares of stock.

A *long-term* capital gain occurs when you sell at a profit stock you have held more than six months. The holding period starts the day after you bought the stock and ends on the day of sale.

A *short-term* gain occurs when you sell at a profit stock you have held six months or less.

You establish a *capital loss* when you sell a stock for less than your cost. A *long-term* capital loss is on a stock you have held more than six months, and a *short-term* loss is on one you have held six months or less.

In order to establish either a capital loss or capital gain on stocks, keep in mind that the proof of the loss or gain depends on your *confirmation slips,* issued by the brokerage house at the time of a purchase or sale.

The key date in establishing a capital gain or loss is the date of the buy or sell order shown on the confirmation slip. The date on the actual stock certificate may be, as was the case in most of 1968, weeks or months later. The confirmation slip date is the one used for putting you on the company's books as a stockholder. It is the date you use for figuring your holding period.

HOW TO FIGURE COST BASE ON YOUR STOCKS

To determine your cost base, divide what you paid for the stock, including the broker's commission and tax, if any, by the number of shares bought.

                                                    Total

50 shares Westinghouse Electric @ 51 + commission $29.90 = $2,579.90

```
         60
      51.59
   50/2579.90      = $51.60 cost base per share
      250
       79
       50
       29 9
       25 0
        4 90
        4 50
```

From time to time you may need to figure your cost base for any of the following reasons:

1. New shares bought in the same company

Figure your cost separately for each batch of shares. It may work to your advantage to sell 20 shares bought at a higher price than 20 shares bought at a lower price. By selling the shares with the higher cost base, you have less capital gain. If you hold shares at a loss, selling those with the lowest cost base will work to your advantage.

2. Stock split

A stock split adds to the number of shares you own, but not to your cost base. In a two-for-one split you have twice as many shares at the same cost, so that each share now has a cost base of half as much as formerly.

3. Stock dividend

Usually a stock dividend adds to the number of shares you

own, but not to your original cost, so you should adjust your cost base, dividing the amount you paid for the stock by the number of shares you now own. The corporation informs the stockholder whether or not the original cost base is increased.

4. Stock rights

If you exercise rights, partly paying for new shares offered you, the amount you pay adds to your cost base. If you choose not to exercise your rights and receive a check from the company for the rights, or if you receive a check for a fractional share, the amount is capital gain and must be reported as such.

If you received stock as an inheritance, your cost base is the price per share on the death date of the one who willed it to you, or the alternate choice, the price one year later.

When you receive shares of stock as a gift, your cost base is the adjusted base of the donor. Be sure to get this information to file with your gift stock certificate.

HOW YOU CAN GAIN BY END-OF-YEAR SALES

Toward the end of the year some investors get uneasy and scramble to sell stocks with capital losses to offset any capital gains they have already taken. This may be a smart move. On the other hand, it may be unwise. The experts remind us that an investor should never sell a security just to improve tax position. Tax savings should always be considered of secondary importance. Improving your portfolio of stocks should be your first objective.

If you have carefully chosen your stocks and are keeping tabs on them, don't sell just to establish a capital loss, even if the stocks are roller-coasting downward at the moment. But if the market and all other indications point to selling your stock, then sell and take your profits.

Perhaps the inflated price of your shares means the yield is less than when you bought the stock. You wouldn't buy more shares at the present price. You would prefer some other stock, but if you unload the stock now, you'd pay high capital gains tax. In this case, no matter how great the capital gains and no matter what the tax, you should sell. You can then invest the proceeds in tip-top stock that will start climbing.

Perhaps you have high paper profits, but you still like the stock. You can sell, take your profits, and immediately re-buy shares of the same stock, thus giving you a higher cost base for future sale. You will, though, be paying extra tax and commissions to your broker, and income tax on capital gains.

Think a moment. Isn't this what investing is all about—to make capital gains? You might as well face the tax fact that you must some day pay tax on any capital gain on stock unless you make a gift of it, or die and leave it to your heirs, or (painful thought) you hold onto the stock until it drops to its original price.

BE SURE TO TAKE ADVANTAGE OF THESE DEDUCTIONS

1. Long-term capital gain

One legitimate way to reduce the income tax you pay is by taking long-term gains, rather than short-term gains. Here's why. A long-term gain results from the sale of a capital asset held more than six months. Only 50 percent of a long-term gain is taxable as income. You add one-half of your capital gain to your regular income—salary, interest, dividends—and pay tax on it all.

A short-term gain, ownership of six months or less, is taxed as ordinary income. You add *all* your short-term capital gains to the rest of your income and pay tax on the total.

2. Capital losses

Capital losses can reduce the amount of income you pay tax on. Capital loss must first be used to offset capital gain. Any remaining loss can then be used to reduce your ordinary income to the extent of $1,000 a year at present.[1] Losses in excess of capital gains plus $1,000 of ordinary income can be carried over indefinitely to future years and used in the same way.

Say you sold stock at a loss of $2,500. You also sold shares in another company with a capital gain of $500. Your capital loss must first be applied to your capital gain of $500. Then $1,000 of the remaining loss can be used to reduce your ordinary income. The balance of the loss can be carried over to the next year and used in the same way.

Warning: A capital loss cannot be claimed if within 30 days before or after the capital loss sale, you buy the same stock. For example, in 1965, suppose you bought 50 shares of Stock G at $60 a share. On November 1, 1968, you sell your 50 shares at $50 a share, a loss of $500. Something happens in the next month and your stock revives, so that on November 26 the stock sells for $58 a share. You decide the stock is a good investment after all and that you would like to get in on the climb. If you re-buy this stock within 30 days of selling it, the government will not allow you a capital loss on the first shares. If you wait to buy new shares until after 30 days have passed, you may use the loss to offset any capital gain and to reduce ordinary income. You can at once reinvest the proceeds in another stock that will go to work for you.

Perhaps you bought shares in Company K at a higher price than the shares sell for today. You see the advantage of taking a capital loss. Still you like the stock, feel it has earning potential and want to keep it in your portfolio. You can do either of these things:

[1] Proposed change in The Tax Reform Bill before Congress at this writing would require $2,000 of long-term capital loss to offset $1,000 of ordinary income.

1. Sell the shares you have, establishing a capital loss, wait 31 days and then invest again in the same stock, taking the chance the stock will not advance too greatly.
2. Buy the same number of shares of the stock you want to sell. Wait 31 days and then sell the first shares, taking the chance your loss will be the same, and establish a capital loss. Or find another company in the same industry and switch when the price is right.

To establish a capital loss during a certain year, you must sell the stock before or on the last business day of the year. To establish a capital gain in a certain year, the sale must be completed and the proceeds available on or before the last business day. Since at present five days are usually allowed to complete a sale, you would have to sell the stock five days before the last day of the year, not counting Sunday or holidays.

Any woman who wants to succeed at investing needs to watch her portfolio constantly. If you find one of your holdings selling for less than your cost price, you probably should sell and establish a loss. Then buy shares of a corporation you have already evaluated and which appears to have a promising future.

NON-BUSINESS DEDUCTIONS

Perhaps you can slice off some of the tax you would otherwise pay by deducting the fee you pay for any of the following:
1. Investment counsel.
2. Renting a safety deposit box for your certificates.
3. Preparation of income tax return.
4. Services of a bookkeeper or accountant in handling your securities.

5. Subscriptions to financial magazines or papers.
6. Subscriptions to investment letters or analyses.
7. State transfer taxes on stocks are deductible. Though often small amounts, they are part of the expense of owning shares and are not added to the cost base.
8. Expense to manage your own portfolio, such as a part of your household expenses—telephone, rent allocated to your office expense.
9. Supplies, stamps.
10. Car expense to and from your broker.

IMPORTANCE OF A WILL

A discussion of taxes would be incomplete without reference to wills. Unless you have made a legal will, with the help of an attorney (this is *not* a do-it-yourself project), you stand in danger of losing a great deal of capital you have worked to protect. In the absence of a will, state officials distribute property according to law, which may not be according to your plans. Often this turns into a costly and lengthy process.

JOINT OWNERSHIP

Many persons believe that by putting all their assets in joint ownership with right of survivorship, they save money and eliminate the need for a will. This may not be so.

There is the chance that both husband and wife may be killed in a common accident. If the state must step in to distribute the couple's assets, the cost is far greater than making wills while both parties were still alive.

Problems arise, too, when a survivor remarries and places her assets in joint ownership with the new husband. Should the woman die before her second husband, he will have the say as to how the money is divided. It may not be the way she or her first husband intended. Joint ownership may also create problems should a couple become divorced.

Legal and estate tax problems may arise when large assets (over $120,000 for a couple, over $60,000 for a single person) are jointly owned. Since laws vary from state to state, you should consult an attorney before making decisions about your estate.

ESTATE TAXES CAN BE REDUCED

As stated in Chapter 13, The Art of Giving, anyone can give away up to $3,000 in cash or property, such as securities, to any number of individuals each year without paying a federal gift tax. In addition to this annual exclusion, the law allows a once-in-a-lifetime gift of $30,000, exempt from gift tax.

Should you, however, make such a gift within three years of your death, the government says the gift was made in contemplation of death. It must be counted as part of your estate for tax purposes.

An older woman who hopes to lighten the tax imposed on her sizeable estate at death, yet wanting her money to last her lifetime, can:

1. Establish a pattern of yearly giving to adult children or to grandchildren, no matter how small the amount.

A woman we'll call Mrs. Chesterton, at her attorney's suggestion, gave her only son $50 a year for five years. She kept a record of the gifts—cancelled checks, and in one case a duplicate stock transfer slip. Then she decided to transfer more funds out of her estate. Taking advantage of the lifetime exemption she gave her son $30,000. Before the year ended Mrs. Chesterton suffered a heart attack and died.

The court ruled that because proof existed that she had established a pattern of giving each year to her son, the $30,000 gift was not made in contemplation of death, even though made within the three-year limit.

2. A woman might also lighten the tax load for her heirs by taking advantage of gifts to charity, retaining a lifetime income. (See Chapter 13, The Art of Giving.)

The heirs of a single woman will have to pay high federal estate and state inheritance taxes. Likewise the heirs of a widow will pay much higher estate taxes, if the estate remains the same, than were paid at her husband's death. Neither heirs can claim the marital deduction of half the estate.

Any estate over $60,000, after deductions such as debts, expenses for last illness and funeral, attorney fees, designated gifts, must pay an estate tax, which rapidly escalates as the estate goes up in value.

Since estate taxes must be paid within 15 months of death of the owner, some provision of cash should be made. To guard against her heirs having to sell stocks or other property at a time of low market value, a woman can provide for such payment by a bank account held in joint ownership with a son or daughter. Another way would be to buy certain government bonds. (Your broker will advise you what kinds.) Bought at a discount today, they would be worth $1,000 each if you die (a special gift from the U.S. government). If you live, you receive the full amount when they mature, and you will, of course, have to pay a capital gains tax.

Though the woman with a large estate can benefit most by understanding how to reduce her estate taxes, those with small holdings also stand to gain. Perhaps right now you couldn't give away even $50. Your property may be too small to be subject to estate taxes. But this may not always hold true. In the future you might be named beneficiary of an estate, or some property you own might sky-rocket in value. It pays to be aware of legitimate tax deductions.

FURTHER TIPS

Keep proofs of your returns—receipts, cancelled checks,

and other evidence to prove your deductions. One investment counselor advises his women clients to keep *all* income tax records, not just for a few years.

Early each year buy a copy of the *U.S. Income Tax Guide.* It sells for $1 on magazine stands. Even though you pay a tax accountant to figure your tax return, you can learn about the figures you need to provide your tax man, some he may not think to ask you about.

Last year an article in a national magazine revealed the search one writer made to get the best deal on his income tax return.[2] He handed identical figures to five different tax return experts and found a spread of $744 between the highest and lowest tax returns. Even after paying all five experts for their work, he still had a savings of $539. Perhaps you can dig up some deductible figures that will mean money in your purse.

Don't let income taxes take you by surprise. Once the broker I deal with helped me see that provision must be made for them ahead of time. I had just sold some stock with a fair-sized capital gain. We talked about replacements and decided on three companies. After figuring up the amount of the new stocks, I said, "That still leaves $1,000 for another company."

"Keep it for taxes," the broker said. Ah, yes! Taxes.

SINGLE WOMEN AT A TAX DISADVANTAGE

The single woman or widow without dependent children must cope with a sizeable tax disadvantage. A married couple receives a "break" by filing a joint income tax return, taking two deductions. When a married man dies, the inheritance tax on his estate can be greatly reduced by the marital deduction. No such favorable tax consideration awaits the estate of the single woman or widow.

[2] Murray Teigh Bloom, "Who Says it's Deductible?", *McCall's,* April, 1968.

A young teacher friend of mine in a high income bracket says, "I figure I work almost two weeks out of every month for the government—welfare, space exploration, and other government spending—taken out before I ever see my pay check."

For this reason women on their own need to keep in mind all the favorable tax deductions and explore every trail that might lead to one. With careful planning many tax dollars can be saved.

How to Benefit Most from This Chapter:

1. Compare the present market price per share of any stock you own with the price when you bought it. Do you have a loser, one that sells for less today than it did several years ago? Can you find the reasons? Should the stock be sold, establishing a capital loss, and a better stock bought?
2. Has one of your stocks leveled off the past year or two and no longer yields as high a rate per share as before? Is this the year you should take your profits and establish a capital gain?
3. Adjust the cost base per share on any stock you own that needs such adjustment.
4. Examine your will to see that it does what you want it to do.
5. If you don't have a will and you own any property or assets you want to pass on to your heirs, see an attorney at once. A simple will, one that will stand up in court, usually costs less than $50.

Beyond Profits   15

Soon after I began to invest in stocks, the market's history aroused my curiosity. How long had our American stock market been in existence? What was it like in those early days? What about other early markets? Did women invest in stocks long age? Did they make any profits? These and other questions bounced around in my mind. What I read and learned about the stock market's fabulous past, its daring adventurers and equally daring shareholders, fortified me to invest in our present-day market.

When Christopher Columbus wildly dreamed of sailing the seas to discover a short route to the Indies, and asked for money for ships and supplies for the venture, he met with stiff opposition. Refusing to give up, he brought his daring cause to Queen Isabella of Spain. She cocked her ear toward the adventurer, offered to pawn her jewels, but finally persuaded the court treasurer to supply the money. Columbus set out in 1492 on his unpredictable voyage. For her financial backing the Queen was to receive a percentage of whatever riches Columbus gained.

The Queen took a tremendous risk, but the outcome was great! If Queen Isabella could offer to risk her crown jewels on such an uncertain business venture, why should we women hesitate to invest in sound American business corporations, those making great discoveries today and even tomorrow? Such growing industries as atomic energy, communications, drugs, electronics, oceanography, to name a few, caught my attention. By choosing reliable companies in any of these industries, a woman would be taking less risk than Queen Isabella, and be more sure of protecting and increasing her own capital.

Reading the next few pages will give you a glimpse of the adventure and excitement of early stock ventures, and show you that women invested in shares long before the advent of American business.

Another early stockholder, Queen Elizabeth I of England, took a risk on adventuresome Francis Drake when he plunged into the unknown. She bought shares of stock, anonymously, to help outfit him for exploring new trade routes.

In 1577 Drake, with five vessels, the flagship only 63 feet long, set out to discover new worlds. When Drake returned, his vessels laden with jewels, silver and gold, his stockholders found themselves wealthy.

In the Middle Ages money-changers set up a trading market on a bridge over the Seine River. Out of this came the Paris Bourse (European term for stock market, literally purse). Another early stock exchange, organized in 1531 in Antwerp, Belgium, sold shares in the tulip business. Again in 1620 a stock company financed the Mayflower's unpredictable voyage to "The New World."

SHARES SOLD TO PAY FOR REVOLUTIONARY WAR

So the idea of selling shares of stock to finance a new venture or even to pay for a war was not entirely new to our nation. Young and struggling for freedom, our country sold shares, or bonds, to raise capital to pay for the Revolutionary War.

AMERICA'S FIRST STOCK EXCHANGE

Soon the need for a market place for trading shares became urgent. In 1792 a group of merchants and auctioneers met under a sycamore tree on Wall Street, New York City, to form our country's first stock exchange, the basis for the present New York Stock Exchange.

Beyond Profits

The story of America's stock market coincides with the story of our country's growth. Cultivation of the nation's great resources—coal, copper, gold, iron, oils, timber, and farmlands—together with the dawn of the industrial age—machinery, railroads, Model T's, business enterprises—pushed our country forward. Without the stock market, though, growth could not have been so great.

THE GREAT CRASH

Success has not always blessed the stock market. Recessions and wars and panics often shadowed it. In the roaring twenties, greed, speculation, lack of federal rules and restraints all precipitated the worst business crash our nation has ever known. One unethical technique of the period was the "pool," since outlawed by the government. Speculators pooled assets, abilities, and reputations to push up the price of a stock. They bought great blocks of stock in a company, artificially shooting the price up. Then they sold, taking the profits, and causing the stock to drop. Such pools broke many a small company, hurling it into bankruptcy.

At that time speculators bought on margin. Conservative estimates place 40 percent of all customers in 1929 as buying on margin. Because the big-time operators bought heavily on margin, the percentage of shares and money traded was, of course, much greater. At that time stocks could be bought by putting up only 10 percent of the price.

Then the big speculators pyramided their profits. That is, with the paper profits of one kinky transaction they scooped in more shares of another and another, or organized their own securities companies. Often they ran up their paper profits to hundreds of thousands and even millions of dollars.

When the market crashed, their profits tumbled like a pyramid of children's blocks. When the market began to plunge the men had to put up cash for what they owed on margin, and often they had to scrape up shares to sell that no one wanted to buy. This meant loss, more loss, and finally ruin.

One such notorious operator created half a dozen of his own securities companies, each piled on top of the other. Money from new shareholders paid the dividends for previous companies. In those days people bought any stock they could get their hands on. Few bothered to investigate; they only wanted a part of the bonanza.

On that day in 1929 when the market collapsed like a flat tire, panicky stockholders sold 16,400,000 shares. That day's volume stood as the record, untopped, until 1968 when 16,000,000 share days became rather common. (The stock market even chalked up, under very different circumstances than in 1929, several trading days in 1968 of over 20 million shares.)

At the end of the year 1929, though, authorities estimated that stockholders had lost over $40 billion. The crash ushered in the Great Depression. Banks failed, businesses closed. People lost every dollar they owned. At the peak of the depression, which lasted well into the 30's, an estimated 12 million persons were out of work. With savings gone, multitudes stood in bread lines.

Out of all this chaos the nation struggled to regain a sound footing. Interdependently the stock market and American business climbed out of the mess.

SECURITIES AND EXCHANGE ACTS

The damper put on stock market credit by the SEC Acts of 1933 and 1934, and later the Investment Companies Act of 1940, protects not only speculators and small investors, but the stock market, too, against a repeat of the 1929 crash.

TRADING SHARES IN EARLY DAYS

Early rules provided that the president call out the names of stocks for trading. Those violating rules or failing to attend a daily session without a good reason were subject to penalties—6 to 25 cents! As the president called out the name of each stock, brokers announced their bids and offers. This had to be done openly, not secretly, a rule that still holds on today's crowded exchange floor.

In 1863 members adopted the name The New York Stock Exchange, and four years later, thanks to Thomas Edison's genius, installed stock tickers. In 1868 memberships, or seats, on the exchange could be bought. In 1871 the call market was abolished in favor of a continuous market. The present NYSE building, erected in 1903, with its great classical pillars stands on Wall Street, New York City, just off Broadway.

THE CURB OR AMEX

Trading on the Curb market began around 1850. Brokers carried on their business outdoors, in all kinds of weather, standing between the curbs of Broad Street, around the corner from Wall Street. Convenient at first when only a few trades a day took place, the method soon developed serious problems. As business increased so did the crowds in the street. Sightseers, traders, and brokers jammed the street, making shouting between clerks and brokers necessary.

WALL STREET

Hub of this nation's securities business, international symbol of American finance, site of some of our country's early history, Wall Street is only three blocks long. Flanked by world famous banking houses, insurance companies, brokerage firms and exchanges, the narrow street runs from Trinity Church to the East River. Skyscrapers 60 and 70 stories high overshadow the solid, more squat New York Stock Exchange Building. Wall Street acquired its name because of a fortified wall the Dutch colonists built as a protection against attacking Indians. At first it was only a primitive trading post where frontiersmen sold bear skins short before they even caught the bears.

LEGENDARY TERMS

Tradition has it that a declining market is called a bear market because of a bear's habit of clawing downward. A rising market is called a bull market because of a bull's habit of tossing his horns upward.

Legend tells us that the rule of stock prices quoted in eighths of a dollar is a throw-backto the early stock trading days of Queen Isabella of Spain when Spanish pieces of eight were in circulation.

MODERN TOUCH

A discount store in Vermont played a new shoppers game when it offered shares of stock in four corporations for its Yuletide gimmick. For the month of December customers registered their guess for the closing price on December 20 of each of the four stocks. The one guessing closest to the stock's actual closing price received the share of stock.

The New York Stock Exchange generally celebrates its birthday in a formal way every 25 years. In 1942, for its 150th birthday, the exchange halted all trading for one hour. Working its way out of the depression years, the Dow Jones industrial average stood at 98.65. Twenty-five years later when the 175th celebration came around, trading halted for only a little over 10 minutes. Business was brisk and the Dow Jones industrials closed for the day at 882.24.

Fabled, fascinating, practical, and relentless, the stock market is an integral part of our nation's business and life.

Women who take the trouble to be informed, who invest in high quality stocks and have the patience to ride out dips and slides and bear markets, will, along with the companies they have invested in, reap profits.

Although this book has discussed extensively working to increase and protect capital, that is, investing for profits, the last conclusion I would want anyone to arrive at is that *profits* stand at the end of the road in my thinking.

Many of us have riches undreamed of a quarter of a century ago. Somehow the idea pops up that if a woman has money she should spend it for bigger and better luxuries. To many, profits mean only more possessions. They forget that half the world goes to bed hungry. Any woman who regards her income and all the money that falls into her hands as a trust will carefully screen her requirements. She will strike some sort of balance between getting and giving.

To protect our own interests, to provide for loved ones, to share with the world, we must not only use our capital with great care, but also take steps to increase it.

Let's recall some steps that will pay off:

Step I—Survey the situation

Today's popular slogan, "She has it made," is just not true for most of us. One thing sure, money is often easier to earn today than to keep or manage. But any woman who capably manages her household accounts or budgets her salary has a fine basis for managing her lifetime capital.

True, we live in a money world, a world of melting dollars and mounting taxes, with the cost of living taking off into space. Many young women are already deep in debt. Many middle-aged women ignore the future, while countless older women have inadequately prepared for their retirement and old age. In some cases this cannot be helped. In his 1968 campaign President Nixon said that social security benefits were much higher in 1968 than in 1958, yet the payee had less to spend because of the rise in taxes and cost of living.

If your preparation for the future is inadequate, it's best to face the fact at once and map out your strategy to change circumstances. Do you fit into any of the following categories?

Wife and mother concentrating in a big way on *today*.
Widow or divorcee with dependent children just squeaking by.

Single girl with everything you own in the clothes closet.

Woman on the brink of retirement unprepared for that state.

If so, you can scramble out. Some women blame their own bad management on bad luck. Bad management can be overcome. It won't be easy, but as an adult, the earlier you consider the major financial requirements of your lifetime—insurance, house, education, emergencies, philanthropy—the closer you'll come on target: *Protecting and increasing your capital.*

Step II—Check spending

If you keep your indebtedness to a bare minimum you're on the way. Some women go through 20 years or more of working, but never get a car paid for. Payments for the new car begin before the old car is fully paid for. More than a few women complacently consider this a form of enforced savings. But when you stop to figure out the amount of interest paid on such transactions, the savings melt away. (The cost of renting money remains high.) Far better to struggle beforehand to bank the money and *collect* interest instead of paying it.

Some while back the lead editorial in *The Wall Street Journal* made this observation:

> ...almost all of us are up from poverty, and almost none of our forebears considered it anybody's responsibility but his own to get up. The pioneer was poor; so was the Irish or Jewish immigrant, the freed slave. For a long time, America as a nation was poor—underdeveloped as they say today.
>
> What transferred general poverty into general prosperity was neither a collective guild complex nor government. It was a lot of individual hard work and a great deal of freedom to move and act and think. Freedom to move not only over the land but also upward as far as ability would carry, freedom to tinker, to invent or refine the innovations of others. Out of it all came the economic organization that has spelled the emancipation from

drudgery, the material abundance, the drastic reduction of poverty.[1]

Of course poverty still is a national problem, but the majority of us have more to spend than our parents and grandparents had.

Step III—Get the savings habit

Do you sometimes overbuy just because you hold a credit card in your hand? Some women are deep in debt simply because it's easy to say, "Charge it," for anything they want. Whether you're the kind that saves by getting dividend checks to the bank before the 10th of the month or the kind who adds a teaspoonful of water to the last of the ketchup in the bottle, changing some of your spending habits to saving habits can add up to profits for you.

Saving regularly can be the take-off for a sound financial position. Consider these ways:

1. Your bank will automatically transfer a regular amount from your checking account to your savings account where it will at once draw interest.
2. If your employer has a government savings bond program, you can buy a bond a month, the amount being deducted from your pay check before you get it.
3. Monthly Investment Plan of the New York Stock Exchange.
4. Mutual funds regular investment plans.

Regular saving is not easy to begin, but once you establish the habit, you won't want to break it. The amount saved is not nearly so important as saving regularly. Decide on the amount you want to save each month and make the payment of it as imperative as rent or house payments. If a bonus or surprise sum of money drops into your hands, run right down to the bank with it.

[1]*The Wall Street Journal,* March 11 1964. Used by permission.

Step IV—Invest in common stocks

As soon as you have a fair sum of money above your current and emergency needs, invest it in common stock shares where the money can grow along with the rising cost of living.

If you want to provide money for the years ahead, then you'll invest in good sound companies. Daily fluctuations of the stock market won't worry you too much. Rather you'll hope for appreciation five, or fifteen years from now.

As you continue to invest your capital you will reap rewards beyond profits. Warm-hearted women often long to give generously. They dream of giving large amounts to the church, of endowing their college, building a hospital, giving food for the world's starving. But they overlook the hard work that comes before the profits that make such gifts possible. In fantasy they just stand there on the platform and give the thousand dollar check (or $50,000). Of course, wealthy women can do just that. But for the rest of us, not blessed with the Midas touch, money must be carefully managed, so that greater profits may be shared.

Certainly not all the methods I found helpful in protecting and increasing money will work for you, but some of them should. One may be just the push you need to get started on skillful investment of your money. Then you can climb the staircase to your own success.

To keep ahead of the plunging dollar, provide income for the future, and share the profits is as provocative as any challenge women face today. Investing in sound, well-managed American companies is an investment in the future—yours!

BIBLIOGRAPHY

Babson, Thomas E. and Babson, David L., *Investing for a Successful Future,* Macmillan Co., N.Y., 1959.

Bradley, Joseph F. and Wherry, Ralph H., *Personal and Family Finance,* Holt & Rinehart, N.Y., 1961.

Brown, J.J., *Start with $100, Common Sense Investing,* G.P. Putnam's Sons, N.Y., 1962.

Campbell, Don, *Understanding Stocks,* Doubleday and Co., Garden City, N.Y., 1965.

Casey, William J., *Mutual Funds Desk Book,* Institute for Business Planning, Inc., N.Y., 1965.

Donaldson, Elvin F. and Pfahl, John K., *Personal Finance,* Ronald Press, N.Y., 1961.

Engel, Louis, *How to Buy Stocks,* Bantam Books, N.Y., 1962.

Epstein, Ralph C., *Making Money in Today's Market,* Ronald Press, N.Y. 1959.

Fisher, Philip A., *Common Stocks and Uncommon Profits,* Harper, N.Y., 1958.

Fisher, Philip A., *Paths to Wealth Through Common Stocks,* Prentice-Hall, Inc., Englewood Cliffs, N.J., 1960.

Friel, Betty, *Decimals and Percentages,* Doubleday and Co., Garden City, N.Y., 1964.

Kahn, Jr., Harry, *A Primer for Profit in the Stock Market,* Doubleday and Co., Garden City, N.Y., 1959.

Lasser, I., and Porter, Sylvia, *Managing Your Money,* Holt and Rinehart, N.Y., 1961.

Levy Herta Hess, *What Every Woman Should Know About Investing Her Money,* Dartnell, Chicago, Ill., 1968.

Loll, Jr., Leo M. and Buckley, Julian G., *The Over-the-Counter Securities Market,* Prentice-Hall, Englewood Cliffs, N.J., 1967.

Merritt, Robert D., *Financial Independence Through Common Stocks,* Simon and Schuster, N.Y., 1954.

Morgan, Alice B., *Investor's Road Map,* Simon and Schuster, N.Y., 1956.

Palmer, Hannah Gardner, *How to Be a Woman of Property,* Henry Holt, N.Y., 1956.

Piper, Otto A., *The Christian Meaning of Money,* Prentice-Hall, Englewood Cliffs, N.J., 1965.

Schultz, Gladys Denny, *Widows Wise and Otherwise*, J.B.Lippincott Co., Philadelphia, Penn., 1949.

Straley, John A., *What About Common Stocks?* Harper & Row, N.Y., 1962.

Tyler, Poyntz, editor, *Securities, Exchanges and the SEC*, H. W. Wilson, 1965.

Wise, T.A., and editors of *Fortune, The Insiders*, Doubleday & Co., Garden City, N.Y., 1962.

Yarmon, Morton, *Invest Smartly*, Charles Scribner's Sons, N.Y., 1961.